DEMON DEALER

A GLIMPSE INTO A DEMONOLOGIST'S SINISTER JOURNEY

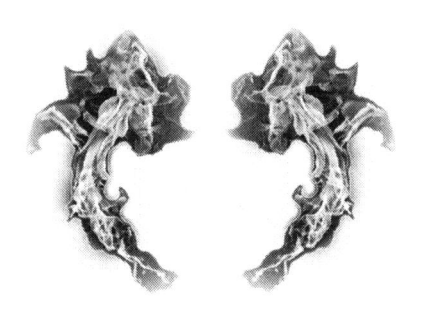

MELINDA KAY LYONS

DEMON DEALER:
A GLIMPSE INTO A DEMONOLOGIST'S
SINISTER JOURNEY

Copyright © 2020 by Melinda Kay Lyons

All portions of this work pertaining to content translation, annotations and notes, original artwork, and any and all other original content, is subjected to copyright. All rights reserved by the Publisher, whether the whole or part of the material is concerned, specifically the rights of translation, reprinting, reuse of illustrations, recitation, broadcasting, reproduction on microfilms or in any other physical way, and transmission or information storage and retrieval, electronic adaptation, computer software, or by similar or dissimilar methodology now known or hereafter developed. Exempted from this legal reservation are brief excerpts in connection with reviews or scholarly analysis. Duplication of this publication or parts thereof is permitted only under the provisions of the Copyright Law of the Publisher's location, in it's current version, and permission for use must always be obtained from Melinda Kay Lyons. Violations are liable to prosecution under the respective Copyright Law.

ISBN: 9781692748418

FIRST EDITION 2020

Publisher: Kindle Direct Publishing
Editor/ Author: Melinda Kay Lyons
Logo Art: LFM Books
Some Cover & Interior Images by: Shutterstock & Depositphotos.com

DISCLAIMER:
The content in hand is intended for educational purposes only. The author/ publisher of this book is not responsible in any manner whatsoever for any adverse effects arising directly or indirectly as a result of the information provided in this book. If not practiced/ used safely with caution, Demonology can be spiritually, emotionally, mentally and physically dangerous to one's health. The concepts and practices presented here are to be used if chosen at your own risk. Melinda Kay Lyons is not responsible for the experiences you obtain from working with the methods presented. The content in this book is based on the author's personal experience and conjecture and published with the intent to only educate and not meant to encourage physical, mental, emotional or spiritual harm.

ALSO BY MELINDA KAY LYONS

DEMONS AND FAMILIARS

DEDICATION

This book is dedicated to those open to the spiritual realm that need a reminder that you're not alone. An attribution to the positive and negative aspects, experiences and spirits, for without their love and brutal affliction, I'd not be the powerful soul I am today.

CONTENTS

INTRODUCTION 9

AWAKENING TO DEATH 17

ELEVEN YEARS LATER 67

HAUNTED INVITATIONS 95

HELLISH RELATIONS 131

PARANORMAL ADVISORY 165

BASED ON A TRUE STORY 219

DEVILISH ENCOUNTERS 267

THE OATH 347

ACKNOWLEDGEMENTS 361

ABOUT THE AUTHOR 363

INTRODUCTION

It's not always a comfortable subject to talk about life after here in a present tense with most folks. In fact, most of my growing up I was taught to believe in the religious aspect of the afterlife through Christian concepts and ideologies, but it wasn't typical for one to question the idea of exactly how the Other Side works, or how one transcends beyond the silver line of consciousness. Not like it was against the rules of the household, but we just simply didn't talk about it much. It was one of those mysteries we for a long time were okay with not knowing much about. And for a long while it seemed alright with them, and it seemed alright with me. Most of those I know are comfortable with the 'not knowing' aspects of the many mysteries of the universe but I was a curious kid with a mind of her own. As I'm sure you've heard that curiosity killed the cat, but it was that statement that drew me to want to learn how and why the cat was killed in the first place. And if I got to those answers, I'd also want to learn where the hell it went after it died. However, in order for one to receive the answers one seeks, one must be in alignment for the universe to construct everything in order for the answers to be revealed. In other words -in order to be in divine alignment, one must be fully ready and prepared for all that is to be revealed for the answers one seeks.

During my teen years, I began having visions and dreams of things I couldn't quite explain. Not typical for one to close their eyes and begin to see swirling lights that waved around my sight similar to that of a light show. This strange phenomenon slowly became a regular art show in my mind's eye the second I lay my head down to sleep and shut my heavy lids. The lights were and still are of a soft glow that seems too transparent for me to see entirely yet are clear as the third eye can see. It wasn't until one night during a sleepover my twin sister Carolyn and I had with one of our neighborhood friends that I asked them about it. As I casually confessed my suspicious night lights, sarcastically both of them responded with either I was crazy, or that there was something wrong with my eyes or brain. Then and there I not only realized I was probably different from others, but that maybe I shouldn't trust each person to completely understand with sincerity of what I was experiencing. It was nearly embarrassing at first, but I decided to shrug it off, turned over and closed my eyes to yet again, another light show.

Not everything is as it seems, nor is it as it should be to what we expect. It's a lot like when you're a child, and you thought you completely understood something, but then eventually learned more about it and realized you knew nothing about it at all. The more I began to learn about spirit from my personal experiences the deeper my understanding got and the more I wanted to know.

PARANORMAL SLUMBER PARTY

Which brings me to my very first paranormal encounter that had me literally jumping out of my skin -or in this case *out of my bed*. Though I'm not sure exactly what age I was, I do know it was around the same time my whole life began to change from the inside out. I still remember this experience like it was yesterday, for the panic that rang throughout my entire body obstructed my ability to even stand due to the amount of fear and anxiety overtaking me. It was in my bedroom on a late afternoon where I was by myself either drawing or studying on Japanese language (because I took it for school thinking I'd be a translator someday for the living *-boy did I get that backwards!*). Nothing too crazy was going on, only that I was spending time alone but during some moment then in my peripheral vision I noticed the bedroom door slowly opened by itself. Intuitively I knew there was something else in the room and it had walked into my room knowing full well I would notice. The idea of a ghost never really scared me unless the spirit itself was intending to be so. Though I never had actually seen an apparition (yet), the thought of seeing or experiencing a spirit didn't frighten me but intrigued me greatly. It was in this moment in my room I decided to entice that curiosity more but what happened next was NOT something I was prepared for.

Gently I made the decision to drop the items I was using to the floor below me. Being an identical twin, my parents had gotten my sister and I a bunkbed, and fearful of the bed falling on top of me, I always took the top -though I always told my sister it was because I wanted the extra exercise. Once the items met the floor that was when I leaned back on my bed where I was originally sitting and nonchalantly invited it to lay or sit next to me. I asked it to be gentle as I positioned with my back on my bed as if waiting for something to occur. It must've been less than five minutes laying there quietly, though quickly I started to think I was crazy after all. But not too long after, it suddenly got cold next to me and it was when I could feel massive amounts of goosebumps overcrowd my arm as the hair on my skin stood up. The second I noticed this change, that was when before my very eyes, I witnessed the mattress on my bed begin to move downward as if a heavy hand or leg mounted the edge of the bed. When this occurred, my body had also moved with the motions of this invisible weight climb on top of me, pinning me down onto the mattress. Though I couldn't see anyone or anything, not a trace of a face, arms or legs, however I could feel massive amounts of energy pushing on my abdomen as if a full body of a man were on top of me. Unable to move my arms, legs or even motion my chest upward, that was when I began to panic. Being that I was raised Christian I instantly remembered being taught to call onto Jesus Christ or Angels for help from bad or negative spiritual encounters. As I called out Jesus' name for help, suddenly the weight was lifted and the moment I felt freedom from this invisible boulder, without hesitation I bolted from my bed, grabbed my Holy Bible that rested on the nightstand and began shouting for it to leave in the name of Jesus Christ. Not sure why I did this, but I think in the moment it was the only type of spiritual protection I knew and wasn't about to let the opportunity of any kind of spiritual help slide by.

I must've stood there at least fifteen minutes telling the spirit to back off. I'd be pacing back and forth in my room yelling telling it to leave me alone, to never touch me again. It was also here that I realized something deeper within myself that I didn't think I had inside of me, and that's the **FIGHTER SPIRIT**. To the observer it would appear as if I were cowering behind a book that was created centuries ago. But in fact, what I wasn't aware of was in that moment it was a possible test of my soul's courage and just how far I'd be willing to go for spiritual self-protection. Was I scared? Hell yea! But at the same time, I was angry at the fact this spirit took advantage of my level of vulnerability and willingness to connect with it. Although I had just experienced what most would call a once in a lifetime of evidence based on the paranormal, I was shook up to the point where I couldn't tell anyone for a few hours. I didn't even have the courage to tell my sister or my mom. Eventually I tried to tell my twin sister Carolyn, but in her expression, I could see she didn't quite believe me, and I was reminded not everyone was going to.

For a few weeks after that I was hugely paranoid of ever being alone in my room again. It eventually came to the point where I began to clutch to Christianity more, for I felt that maybe because of my freedom from the invisible force, that perhaps there was some truth to the religion after all. I started reading the Bible but didn't really read past the section of Genesis for lack of a better word, I got bored of repetitive phrases and lack of full answers to my many questions. Eventually I was invited to attend church with my girlfriend down the house from us, and reluctantly I declined but soon enough gave in and went a few times. Not a fan of church nor am I a fan of the idea that we should share our most embarrassing moments of our lives to a total stranger in front of the entire church, or even remotely at all in private.

Though there was still some sore inside of my heart that made me feel there was still some ounce of truth to this intimidating, yet frightening book, that has instilled hope and even fear to millions. Each moment I'd grace with the tip of my thoughts along with my fingers over the many pages that didn't seem to add up, but that was when I began to develop more complicated questions. I still remember a moment where I was back in my bedroom, yelling at God asking for the answers. Almost to the point where I was demanding them. Picking up the black leather ancient text with both hands, raised them up to whoever invisible from above was observing to see the desperation of my demands.

Nay to the silly human that ever commands or demands anything from the higher power that created you many would say, but I didn't care anymore for I felt I deserved to know why, how and where I came from, and to learn what the purpose was to our own existence. No longer was I satisfied with the sugarcoated tall tales of a single man and woman that created all of humanity, but was now in the ambitious mission to understand the spiritual and human condition. After what felt like thirty minutes alone in my room yelling at nothing, little did I know that something and someone heard me and that I'd be on a journey to receiving exactly what I wanted to know and **more**.

MELINDA KAY LYONS

Awakening to Death

I'm a firm believer that you never really understand nor respect the idea of something until you've fully experienced it for yourself. No matter how outlandish or cruel it may be, one cannot judge something by simply looking at it from an outside perspective. Although there are obvious things we can observe and know naturally without question that something is bad or unhealthy, for we as psychic beings, can sense energetic impacts intuitively through the negative and positive messages our senses receive. However, sometimes there's going to be subject matters that may seem evil to the naïve or ignorant but that's only because one hasn't simply experienced it for themselves to fully comprehend exactly what, or how it all works. In the topic of communicating with the dead, I've encountered my fair share of doubters and skeptics. Most often I receive the every so often, "You've never flatlined in a hospital, so you don't know anything about the dead or the other side." Let's not forget the other side of the coin of the religious believer carrying doubt on their back, "It's against God and the Bible to be connecting with the dead. What you do is wrong and of the Devil" Adding the icing on the cake, the condemning Christians or those of their chosen faith… "I hope you know you're going to Hell when you die because it's a sin to do what you do."

As tempting as it is to dish my own smart comebacks, I've been humbled many times through many different spiritual experiences and ones of this life to know they just don't get it and more than likely never will. So why bother trying to convince the man or woman that yells nay when it's plain to see they will only deny what they simply don't understand. It's not within the nature of humans to fully comprehend everything of a topic, that is unless, we've fully embarked on the journey ourselves. Sure, there's moments where I want to give some of these doubters, and even haters a piece of my mind (I *will* if necessary), but I've learned, one must choose their battles in order to remain focused on winning the war ultimately. For we are in a spiritual warfare that's been going on for eons that most of the living simply just don't know is actively happening all around them. Though the awakening process can be scary and even a bit shell shocking, it's a process we all eventually go through once the soul is ready to unveil the 3D illusions and awaken their psychic awareness to the mystical world we've been living with all along. It may seem like to some that what I do is against a God that protests against the adventures of the soul, but it wasn't something I journeyed into on purpose necessarily. In fact, I didn't plan this at all and only wanted to learn about the other side, but wasn't aware just exactly if, or how those answers to my questions would arrive. Never did I expect in a billion years that my life would turn out the way it did, nor did I think even for a minute in utter belief that I'd also be receiving the exact answers to all of my eternal questions.

Near-Death Experience

It all started at a boyfriend's house where we watched tv and kissed like there was no tomorrow. It was summer vacation, we had no homework, nothing to do except explore the world and our raging hormones when his dad wasn't home (sorry mom and dad). How carefree I was in this time of my life. Though I worked hard at being a straight A student (tried) and the overindulgence of friends, video games, music and art, however I wasn't one to be very educated nor aware of certain health concerns or warning signs. Neither him, nor I knew what hives were. But they most certainly were beginning to spread all over my body, followed with itching and un unexpected heatwave that started to make me sweat.

We were hanging out at my boyfriend John's house while enjoying the time spent together with no plans of our day. And it was in the moment of quality time where John couldn't help but take notice after we had lunch, that something strange was developing all over my arms and face. A red rash seemed to begin spreading along my arms, neck, chest, stomach and legs. Unsure of what this was, we thought maybe it would just go away and went outside for a bit to get some fresh air by taking a walk. Not shortly after we strolled for a walk, an unsuspecting truck pulled up beside us and the head to appear from the driver side window was my grandmother, Maryann. She spotted us just outside right when we were having our stroll in the summer sun that she then asserted herself to ask what was going on with my body. Telling her that I hadn't a clue, she then asked what I had eaten before this suspicious rash occurred. It took me a moment before I remembered and said,

"Well I had eaten a hotdog with bits of cheese in it that I haven't had before -but I've always eaten beef."

Still unsure what the mysterious rash was, she told me to wash my body with soap and water. As she drove away, I went back into my boyfriend's house to do just that, but nothing seemed to change. In fact, it looked as if within minutes the heat from the water made it worse, causing my legs and arms to get even hotter and redder. I remember taking off my maroon high school hoodie I always wore and being so glad that sucker was off before I'd pass out from what felt like a soon-to-be heatstroke. Not an hour had passed and by this time my face had large splotches of red lumps all over including my body. Some of these hives were getting so large that some were as *big as my hand*. It was when John's concern grew and encouraged that I call my grandmother, so I did.

She then surprisingly said we had a doctor in the family that happened to be visiting her house that day, whom I never met before, nor heard of. After he heard what my grandma told him, he urged her to hand him the phone to tell him of my symptoms. After about three minutes describing the details, he asked,

"Does your throat feel funny? Are you having a hard time swallowing?"

I then did a few practice attempts and responded,

"Yeah. It's hard to swallow now noticing, which is a bit weird."

His tone was suddenly professional and ordered with haste, "-*You need to call 911 now. If you don't, you'll die.*"

Explaining to my teenage mind of eighteen, that hives were not only spreading all over the outside of my body, but also internally which causes the throat to close, giving the person anaphylactic shock that makes them suffocate. Honestly, I thought this guy was crazy and was probably exaggerating it like my grandma. But the way in how he said it, and what he said, ran chills run down my spine that I'll never forget. It suddenly reminded me that I was mortal and what he was saying could very well be the truth and I was in a heap of trouble. So, to ease my grandmother's worry and honestly my own, I listened to this guy and dialed 911.

I can only imagine how dumb I must've sounded on the other end of the line when I made the call. For once the person on the other end answered saying,

"...911 what's your emergency?"

I then said while trying to remain calm...

"...Yeah, my grandma said I should call you because she and a relative are saying if I don't, I'll die -but I think they're just blowing it out of proportion." (Love you grandma).

Then the person taking notes asked what my situation was, and I told her what was going on. After explaining to her in brief detail of my health, she said just to be on the safe side, they'd send an ambulance to check up on me to evaluate the situation pronto. But in the meantime, she instructed that I get a cold cloth and put it to my head because too much heat to the brain can damage the braincells.

Without delay, John grabbed a hand towel damped it with cold water, and I placed it on my head. It only took them about five minutes for the ambulance team to arrive through the front door.

Now naturally being eighteen, I wasn't against the idea of four handsome men in uniform surrounding me but the look of the EMT's faces when they entered the house was evidence of just how serious this was. For as soon as they saw me their speed *quickened*. I can still clearly recall one of them stopping in his tracks nearly gasping when he saw how red my face was. Thinking on it now, I was in terrible shape that even I can't believe how bad it really was. My face was covered, my entire body was covered from head to toe in massive sized hives. I can only imagine how frightened these amazingly helpful people were. I of course, didn't understand at the time just how life threatening this was, but the moment I took notice of the individual reactions, it was evident it wasn't a joke. Each person was doing their thing with tubes, needles and whatever else that was necessary to save my life. It only took a few seconds for anxiety to consume me as both of my legs were shaking up and down guided with nervous anticipation. Being as I've never had something like this happen to me before I wasn't sure what to expect, but it was obvious it was more serious than I had anticipated.

One of the EMT's positioned himself in front of me guiding me along the process of what was happening while asking me, now the third time, of the same question…

"Do you know what you ate today Melinda? Did you eat something you haven't eaten before?"

Giving him the same answer but this time my nerves were nearly shot for I couldn't stop shaking within my whole body. It wasn't hard to see that I was now scared for my life, but I had to trust that these men knew what they were doing.

"-I…ah hate -ate a…ought -hotdog I hadn't had before with cheese in it.."

He nodded in response to my answer while now pumping my arm with what he said was Benadryl. This moment he told me,

"Melinda, it's uncertain exactly what's causing your hives, but we're going to do everything we can to stop it. Your body is having an allergic reaction to something and this medicine is going to help it. But we need you to try your best to remain calm."

His voice soothed some of the fear, but it wasn't stopping it completely for I began to have trouble breathing and said,

"I can't breathe."

The same EMT sitting in front of me then handed me a brown paper bag while reassuring me that I could be experiencing an anxiety attack, for they can feel similar to a heart attack. Saying it was best to breathe slowly into the bag to ease the nerves. Though I did what he had confidently instructed, while inhaling and exhaling, observing how my breathing was bringing the paper bag in and out, but it wasn't helping. The next thing I can remember is saying in utter fright was,

"-I can't breathe!"

It was then I just remember suddenly feeling like I was on the moon unable to inhale. I was now in desperate need of air and I began clawing and grabbing my throat violently like some kind of savage animal to what may have seemed like a hopeless attempt for life again. In order for them to prevent me from harming myself, each EMT quickly restrained my arms and legs and pinned me to the couch in the living room where they found me. Each eye gazed upon my now aggressive shaking anticipation to breathe. My body was flinging from hope that each plunge may miraculously bring me back to earth again, but to no avail. I'll never forget the look of terror in my boyfriend's eyes as tears of what seemed to be his worst nightmare as he helplessly witnessed what he thought would be the end of me. It felt as if oxygen itself had rejected my lungs and refused any ability to capture a grace of freedom from the closed walls of my airway.

It all happened so fast. The best way I can describe this next part is I just remember the feeling of final surrender to the suffocation and knew I wanted *out*. I wanted out of this position of helplessness and I wanted to be free from it all. It was in this inner desire to escape that soon evolved to a destination, which led my soul to swiftly jump out of my temporary shell that now laid dormant on the sofa. My eyes weren't even closed I don't think. I remember the overpowering lust to jump out. That's when slowly yet ever so quickly without frustration, I felt my soul energy of consciousness and awareness leave my body. This was the moment I feel was my near-death experience that also led me to my first **ASTRAL PROJECTION** experience at the same time.

ASTRAL PROJECTION

IS A MOTION WHERE THE SOUL ESCAPES THE PHYSICAL BODY. ALSO KNOWN AS OBE, OR OUT-OF-BODY EXPERIENCE, WHERE THE SOUL (CONSCIOUSNESS) TEMPORARILY, INTENTIONALLY DEPARTS THE BODY AND TRAVELS THROUGHOUT THE UNIVERSE AND ON THE ASTRAL PLANE.

DEMON DEALER

I remember gazing around me and saw other light beings smiling at me with nothing but a soft peacefulness that seemed to illuminate from their eyes. It was here I also realized I was still in the house, but now standing behind the couch. And it was here, where I saw the other living people trying to save my life but were now quiet as they observed my motionless body not responding nor breathing. I'm not sure how long I was in this moment of speechlessness, but without wasting time the souls that I didn't recognize began to speak to me through telepathy.

What I've learned is not all folks that have a near-death experience will immediately communicate with the dead through telepathy, but that was how it was for me. Surprisingly I was okay with it to the point where I felt like it was totally normal to me. Almost like I had been waiting for this for a very long time but couldn't explain where this sense of belonging came from. During our communication I would notice that these departed souls were transparent and solid at the same time while glowing similar to like a million stars inside or a part of them. Their very presence was comforting, though most of them didn't speak but merely observed with a soft smile. The ones that did speak to me seemed to have a peace within each phrase and word transferred from their mind to mine, which enabled my anxiety to suddenly vanish. Feeling completely secure and safe in this experience without feeling any amount of fear or loss.

One soul in particular, a male energy, told me they had been watching me for a long time and that I'd be able to explore the other side if I so choose. Calmly they walked me over to the couch where I stood beside my body and watched as John was now shedding tears of urgency for me to come back. As I felt a hand on my shoulder, the male energy told me I can either leave (die) or stay. I knew in this instance that I wasn't ready to die, for the last thing I wanted was to leave my family, friends and miss out on all of the possibilities of my life. I was only eighteen, I wasn't ready to end it yet. As I expressed this to this male soul, he then said it was fine and it was my choice but that I'd have to go back right away.

It was also here in the moment I realized how crappy I looked laying there. "God, I look like Hell."

There and then I heard laughter from the once muted souls fill the space of this Astral experience. I then said,

"Wait. So, our bodies aren't a part of the soul at all? The body is super heavy yet, when I'm out, I feel like I didn't lose any part of me. I actually feel more whole."

With an even bigger grin he nodded, "Yes! It's almost like you're wearing a giant meat suit."

We all laughed at this idea. Although some would be satisfied with just a mere hello and goodbye, they could sense almost instantly that I wanted to return to my body but didn't want to miss out on learning more *-so much more*. That's when the male soul reassured me that once

I had returned to my body, they would help me again to Astral Project as I slept, in order to have further questions answered.

Though this experience seemed exceedingly long, I was only without air for a few minutes. The male soul said he would help me go back into my body, and at first it would be a little difficult for me to do on my own. That's when I remember climbing on top of the shell of my borrowed human self to become parallel over my now accepted meat suit. Almost instantly my frail lifeless body suddenly gasped for air granting the innate ability to use the now opened airway to inhale and exhale once again.

MY FIRST ASTRAL PROJECTION

Though this was an extensive experience that goes into even greater detail, I had ended up completely forgetting much, if not all of it for the next eleven years of my life. What many didn't know and what I had forgotten for that timeline was I had actually met Jesus Christ during the following astral projection that same day immediately after my near-death experience. It was when I was on the way to the hospital where I began to see a bright light emerge from the walls of the ambulance and neither the EMTs could see what I was witnessing.

"Wow, is there really a white light when we die?" I said aloud not minding they were writing notes of my hospitalization needs.

One of the EMT's then placed his hand on the wall of the vehicle, to show that there was no light.

I then lifted a now very heavy arm and said, "No. I'm serious. I see a white light similar to a rainbow."

Then that's when I started to also see butterflies emerge from this beautiful white light emanating and manifesting before my very eyes and no one else could see it but me. However, to discourage this amazing experience, the EMTs remained rational explaining the effects of the medicine can cause hallucinations. But I didn't care for then I could begin to hear music, a hymn echoing a beautiful whimsical tune within my very ears and that's when I heard the voice of what for a long time, I thought was God.

Not to focus too much on this portion because respectfully it's a very long experience to explain in justified detail -but what I can tell you is for a long time when I learned of this God entity speaking to me, that it wasn't a God that's depicted in the Bible, but energies much more humbling, loving and relatable. During the same astral projection, I had also met Jesus Christ, Mary Magdalene, divine Angels and many other amazing benevolent spirits where they took me to what appeared to be similar to a Heaven plane. They had surrounded me with immense amounts of love and healing energy that could change even the most doubtful of skeptics. But what strung my heartstrings the most, would be when I was reunited with my beloved parakeet, Sweety, for she had passed away in my hands just before this drastic life change occurred.

Her soul appeared to me with beautiful blue wings, and rainbow eyes that sparkled like the ocean waves. She even spoke to me in telepathy telling me how we and all other beings are not long gone after death and that she would forever love me as I will always love and miss her.

Being eternally grateful for this magical experience, yet for the longest time I completely forgot it all. What I did, was somehow caused myself to have a temporary amnesia that blocked it completely from memory when I made the internal decision to never speak to anyone about it again. For I believed that maybe it was just all a hallucination or a dream like the doctors and many others would suggest after all. No matter how many times I tried to tell someone about these memories, everyone kept looking at me as if I had two heads, and that's when I somehow consciously decided to shove it down into my subconsciousness.

What caused my memory of this transcending experience to reemerge is a whole other story that we will get to very soon.

What needs to be noted is that all of how this went about somehow was in divine timing, for it all was absolutely necessary in order for me to be ready for where my life was ultimately headed. And it was **YEHOSHUA/ YESHUA** *(Jesus Christ's original name, also known* *as Joshua in Hebrew*) that guided me, saying that when I'd remember everything, it would be when the universe knew I was ready.

Hell and Heaven

During my astral projection there was a point where during my meeting with Yehoshua that he had told me many things that I had for a very long time wanted to learn and understand. One of the bigger questions I had was the concern for our eternal fate in the afterlife, and whether or not souls were judged. It was tiring and soul clenching when he revealed to me that the truth is, there is no Hell that people are damned or forced to by a God, and that it's all based on our level of consciousness and how we perceive ourselves that condemns one to a certain fate or destiny on the other side.

It wasn't easy to hear to say the least. In all honesty it frankly pissed me off so much because all I could think about was the fact that bad and terrible people that murder and do horrible acts basically get away with it when they die. There would be no justifiable placement for the souls that hurt others intentionally. As if there was no eternal or soulful justice. That's what it suddenly felt like, and as I heard this, tears and anger overthrew all of my emotional baggage around inside of me. Thankfully he was as calm as one would expect and never broke his serenity within himself and allowed me to process the emotions as best as I could because after all, I was still a teenager.

This doesn't mean there isn't a Hell realm. Hell, and Heaven most *definitely exist*, but not in the way the Holy Bible teaches.

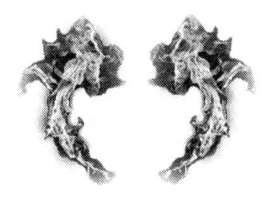

RIGHT AWAY YOU MIGHT BE THINKING I WAS TRICKED BY A MALEVOLENT SPIRIT THAT APPEARED AS THIS JESUS CHRIST FIGURE, IN HOPES TO CONSPIRE AGAINST MY SOUL'S FATE. AND WHY WOULDN'T YOU? YOU WERE PROBABLY TAUGHT THIS FROM THE HOLY BIBLE SAME AS I.

Most of the persons I meet, they share this exact reason of why I'm wrong and that what I've connected with wasn't a positive spirit, but instead was the Devil deceiving me. But what solidified my convincing was he also explained that there is a Hell realm, but not one we are *judged* or *forced* to go to by a loving God like spirit. Instead, it's a realm we can choose to travel to or remain within by the **UNIVERSAL LAW OF FREE WILL**. In its entirety, expressed by Yehoshua, that each living person and those departed are able to be where they choose by the soul's energetic decision based on what they feel they want or what they feel they deserve. When you take a moment to ponder this reality, this would suggest that the power of our emotions can easily transcend us to a place of powerful love and peace, or into a place that is filled with nothing but terror and pain that is triggered by fear.

Not to think for a moment I wasn't still very hurt by this new information, for my mind was still grasping that somehow this meant a loss of justice for those and myself from painful experiences. Shortly after I took in this new and at first, disturbing information, Yehoshua asked,

"What's going on in your mind as you're crying?"

After taking a few seconds to take in the sorrow and mourn from the old thinking, it was then I realized I was crying actual diamondlike tears. Yehoshua remained silently still as I examined this remarkable discovery. As I looked at my hands that seemed to shine while the residual sparkles fell from my too bedazzled pupils, confused yet amazed while still gazing at the diamonds,

"I'm crying sparkles or diamonds? How is this possible? Is this for real?"

Several of the other souls among us too gave a soft reassuring grin as I continued to examine this remarkable evidence. Casually because of course he's known this for centuries, in this moment Yehoshua continued by saying...

YEHOSHUA:

"Right now, we are in a place that many would consider Heaven. There are Heaven dimensions and there are Hell dimensions, but they're based upon how one feels in the moment, or how the many vibrationally feel at one time that are in the same dimension. You're here in this moment because we've helped you ascend to this realm that's focused on healing and love. The tears you're shedding are the energy vibrations you are, which is why they glisten like diamonds because we're stardust."

ME:

"Wow, that's so cool that we're really a part of the universe like this! It's like being a superhero. -But what about the Bible? Are you saying the Bible is all wrong? Is it all just a big lie?"

YEHOSHUA:

*"The Holy Bible isn't a lie but it's not all based on truths either. It's based on some truths but it's not all true. And more than half of what's described in the Bible **never** happened. More than half of the characters in the stories never existed and most of what is described of the many miracles I allegedly performed -never happened and are not true. I never turned water into wine, and I could never walk on water. But...my death is described quite accurately and that's one thing about me that is true."*

My eyes must've been like a deer in headlights at this point. I can only imagine my expression when he told me this. I was completely blown away and also so enticed to want to learn more.

At this moment I started talking to him about my past and of all of the pains and hurts I had experienced. But the one thing that was exceptionally difficult to confess was when I was eight years old. My parents had trusted a certain family member and let him into our home but within a few weeks of his stay, he had molested me. Ever since that night I had felt like God and Angels, or even Heaven had forgotten me. There were many times where I was convinced that from the teachings of the Bible, that maybe it was a punishment from previous sins. That night I had changed into someone else and closed off from many people and knew instantly those closest to you will hurt and take advantage of you without any warning or mercy. Sharing this backstory was exceedingly difficult, even on this realm, because I was sharing it with someone, I had only met for a few minutes. But I knew sharing this pain would help me to heal and move forward. And it was in this experience where he taught me the importance of forgiveness and what it really means.

YEHOSHUA:

"Forgiveness isn't about letting the other person have permission from what they've done to you. It's not about giving them a free card and letting them off the hook. It's about processing the pain, the hurt without apologies and

*allowing yourself to be free from the pain they've caused. I know forgiveness isn't easy, and it can be scary at first for you feel like you're having to let go of the unfair happenings. But that's not what forgiveness is about. It's about, for-giving-yourself freedom from the past. What he did wasn't right and shouldn't have happened, but you also must know, that people that are hurt, confused or are unaware of their actions will simply do what they already know. They won't be aware of the said consequences of their actions, instead will do it simply because it's what they were conditioned with. This doesn't give him or those that do bad and terrible things an excuse, but it does explain **why** they do these things, which can make it easier in the process of forgiveness."*

The more he spoke about forgiveness it truly enabled me permission to be okay with not hating myself, the man that committed the crime or about what happened. More importantly, for not allowing it to hinder my ability to trust others again. But trust is a gift earned, that shouldn't be given to just anyone just because they expect it. There are many immeasurable gifts from the soul that aren't to be taken for granted, but throughout my journey in these countless experiences like these, I've understood to never underestimate your ability to heal and move forward.

However, the concept of Hell not being forced onto a human soul that does intentional harm, still didn't feel fair or right to me -and he could easily sense this within my energy frequency. That was when he continued…

YEHOSHUA:

"…If it will ease your feeling of any injustice, there is a thing called **KARMA** that does and will impact him later in life or in the next life (afterlife). Karma is an energetic balance that corresponds to what we give and what we shall receive in return. When you are loving to someone, you shall receive love in return from either the same person, or from another. If you take from someone selfishly, then you shall most absolutely get your comeuppance. Everything in the universe is balanced by a give and take exchange and it allows you and the other person to receive what you so deserve. Lastly but profoundly, is there is a process called **LIFE REVIEW** and it enables what he did to fully experience the pain he caused you by living through your experience. But not just the one instance, he will also experience the aftermath of how it negatively impacted your life from the relationships like how you struggle with trust again or being vulnerable. Eventually the hurtful things we do to someone else will come back to us like a mirror effect. Though one may do bad or hurtful things without being aware they're doing it, doesn't mean they still won't harvest the understanding from the lesson eventually. All that transpires from our singular moments will be gifted with an even greater knowledge and awareness of thyself. Life is about lessons in both good and bad moments but it's from learning the lessons that make us ascend to a higher level in love, that which brings us closer to ourselves and to others."

How refreshing this information was in being justified in knowing that at least he and others will eventually learn from the lesson. However, there are still sometimes one may doubt if the negative things people really do will come back to them -but I can tell you Karma is certainly a ***real*** cosmic response to all that is energy. Speaking this from receiving my own Karma, and too observing how others also are dished theirs. But Karma isn't meant to be viewed as a sense of revenge, but as a cosmic-like sense of justice that is best well served with faith that it will go as it must in order for the lessons to be learned.

Although this would suit even the most skeptical of individuals, there still remains these heavy questions…

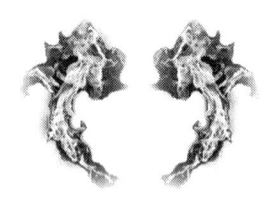

WHAT ABOUT THE PEOPLE THAT NEVER LEARN THE LESSON AND STILL COMMIT THE SAME CRIMES OR DO EVEN WORSE THINGS? WHAT HAPPENS TO THEM? WHERE DO THEY GO? WHAT DO THEY BECOME?

Though Yehoshua was more than wonderful in granting me this unmistakable precious gift to experience, this information was only a small portion of what I was in store for next. As we were coming to a close of our grand meeting, there was another question that frankly worried me, and he knew it was coming...

ME:

"...As amazing as this all is, why am I here? Am I dead? I don't want to die yet, I have so much to live for."

YEHOSHUA:

"You have been brought here for a purpose and one that I and the many of us feel from the course of things that you would take and would do well in."

ME:

"… What do you mean, *purpose?*"

YEHOSHUA:

"If you're willing, I and many other beings would be grateful if you'd take this information and deliver it to others on earth. You have a choice: to die or to return to your family. The choice is yours. But you must know, that the information I'm giving you won't be easy to deliver to most. In fact, it will be a very difficult task and your life will be filled with much struggle, but it will help many people."

Here I was given what seemed like maybe already a few hours into our conversation, but I knew deep down that it wasn't much time in comparison back on earth. I began to think of my family, remembering those I love and how much I was still too young and didn't want to miss out on where my life would or could lead. Plus, come on -it's *freaking Jesus Christ asking me of all people to do this!* But, still… I knew that what he was saying about *"struggle"*, would mean I would suffer much judgment and other situations that would be beyond my control. And that's where it led me to my next question…

ME:

"… Okay I'll go back to earth and do what you're asking me. I feel like if I don't, I'll never know what could've been and the last thing

I'd ever want to do is leave my family. I love them too much that I don't think I could truly leave them this soon. But what's going to happen to me? I mean…how will I convince people that I'm telling the truth? You know as well as anyone, that if I tell others that the Holy Bible isn't correct, they'll call me a liar or something like the antichrist. What do you suggest I do?"

At this present moment his eyes changed to a much deeper sense of pride and hope, and it was easy to tell he was eager to see what I'd say. The following instructions he laid out for me were not something I was initially prepared for. Honestly, I thought he was asking the wrong person for the job. I'm terrible at public speaking, I deal with stage fright and not to mention I look like a kid to most folks, so anyone taking me seriously was going to be a challenge.

YEHOSHUA:

"I'm so glad to hear it Melinda. This is really going to help so many people. But what you must always remember, is you're not trying to get people to believe you. This mission isn't about converting those into your understanding. Instead, your purpose is to help those that are already awakened to these concepts, or those that are ready to receive the messages. Those that will doubt will be the souls not necessarily ready to take in the information because not everyone is on the same level of awareness or consciousness."

ME:

"I see. I understand what you mean. What you did for humanity by trying to help others was so brave, and I'm always forever grateful for the sacrifice you did for everyone."

YEHOSHUA:

"Remember when I said that not all things in the Bible are true? This includes the concept of me saving people through my death. I died because back then people were fearful of what I was teaching and were against the methods of love I was trying to share. Yes, in a way I risked my life for what I was sharing to others, but it was never meant to happen to rescue anyone's soul or to "save" anyone like the Holy Bible describes. And this is what I'd like you to tell others. The Biblical ways are not satisfying the soul's questions any longer and it's time for others like yourself, to deliver the modern approach to eternal salvation -the truth. But don't worry, you won't die like I did."

There was much more discussed between the Middle Eastern Ascended Master and I, but what's struck me in shock was eventually he told me where my future would go and that eventually I would forget all of this experience for the next eleven years.

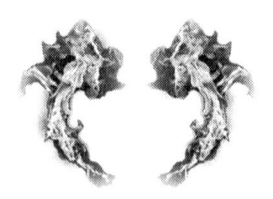

ELEVEN IS A VERY POWERFUL NUMBER IN NUMEROLOGY, FOR IT'S A HIGHLY SPIRITUAL NUMBER, BALANCING THE INTUITIVE QUALITIES OF THE HIGH PRIESTESS WITH LEADERSHIP AND CREATIVE QUALITIES OF THE MAGICIAN. IT IS UNDERSTOOD THAT THOSE WHOSE LIVES ARE INFORMED BY THE NUMBER 11 ARE BOTH SPIRITUALLY SENSITIVE, COOPERATIVE, INDEPENDENT AND CHARISMATIC. NOT SUGGESTING I'M NOW SOME HIGH PRIESTESS, BUT WHAT I AM SAYING IS THIS NUMBER AND ALL THINGS THAT MOVE ALONG WITHIN THE UNIVERSE MOVE INTO DIVINE ALIGNMENT WHEN THE MOMENTS ARE NECESSARY FOR THE NEXT STEPS OF TRANSFORMATION FOR ONESELF AND FOR OTHERS THAT ENCOUNTER THEM.

Just before I went back to my body in the hospital where I was sound asleep, I remember watching my family and noticing how clear everything was. Though I was nothing but pure energy, I could still feel everything and even more! The colors, the sounds, the emotions and not to mention that amount of discouragement I had looking again at my exhausted sleeping self (I definitely needed a tan). But before I could go back, it was in this prominent memory where Yehoshua stood with me and other souls and helped me open my third eye. Here he taught how it would help to keep the connection to the other side and most importantly, to continue to receive information to help humanity.

As the few spirits surrounded me, it was in this instance he placed his finger onto the center of my forehead. Like a cosmic wave, I could see, hear and feel colors, vibrations and things around me clearer. It was such a powerful transition that I swear it almost felt like I was born again. The best way to describe it was something like a big bang of psychic awareness. I still remember how excited I was when my third eye was opened because I couldn't stop shouting how awesome it was like a kid at a toy store. I was even high fiving some of the guys that were with me cheering on my sudden psychic puberty. It was like I instantly was given permission to feel my own inner power that I always dreamed of. Once the opening of my third eye was complete, Yehoshua asked me a question…

YEHOSHUA:

"Melinda, I hope you know that this is going to be really good for many people. You are doing a very selfless thing and we are all going to guide you along the way. But do you have any more concerns before we say goodbye for now?"

I swear, it was like he read me like I was an open book. No one has ever been able to understand me as much as he ever did, and I was so grateful. However, he was right on, for I did have another question, but it lingered more like doubt…

ME:

"I just don't understand why you're asking me to do this. There are so many other people that would do a way better job. I seriously think you're asking the wrong person. What if I mess up? What if I disappoint you? *What if I don't succeed and it was all for nothing? What if I fail?*"

It was at this point where I was in tears again. I couldn't stand the immeasurable idea of a remote possibility that he and all of these caring souls risk so much for me, only to fail them. Almost immediately he placed a gentle touch on my shoulder as many of the other souls did as he replied softly but ever so confidently…

YEHOSHUA:

"I know this seems scary right now. But we and the universe wouldn't have given you this opportunity if you weren't right for the mission. There are many souls we ask for this type of thing, but yours is a special case because it's tailored to your own unique style and that's why we're confident that you're going to be successful. Failure is inevitable. We always face failure at some

point in our lives but as long as you keep pushing forward and never cease to try then you're never truly failing. Failure only occurs when one decides to give up and we know you don't give up easily. We will be watching you all the way and won't forget your time when you begin to remember. All we ask is that you have faith in the universe -in us. Do you have faith in us Melinda?"

ME:
"… Yes of course I do."

YEHOSHUA:
"Then you have nothing to fear."

Without a shred of doubt, Yehoshua smiled bigger in that moment. His confidence was unmistakable. As all of the rest of the most promising of guides that stood alongside me confirmed his comforting statement, I was then placed back into my body for the second time and almost instantly awoke to finding all of the female faces of my immediate family staring down at me.

Melinda Kay Lyons

Near-Death Experience Diary Entry

> Friday age 18 5/19/05
> 53
>
> Dear Diary,
> alot has happened alot. Just last saturday I ended up going to the hospital because of a bacterial reaction. My skin began to get hives, really big, wide, red, hot/warm, hives. John was there the whole time, he was even crying because he was worried, everyone was worried. I was taken to the Hospital by the ambulance, they gave me an I.V. of ~~Benadryl~~ Benadryl, and ~~then they~~ gave me oxygen because ~~I~~ all of a sudden couldn't breathe. I couldn't stop shaking at all, and I had no idea ~~what~~ what →

DEMON DEALER

54

was wrong with me, so I was freaking out at the same time. Mom, Grandma, Sharon, Caralyn, and John were there for me at the hospital. John was really worried, I didn't know that he was that scared for me. I had no idea that he cared for me that much. I think that day made him closer to me, alot closer. He stayed with me for the whole week, just staying at the house, watching t.v., just there to be beside me. He knew that he didn't have to, I told him that he didn't have to, but he said that I was crazy. Basically in his

MELINDA KAY LYONS

55

words, that means that he wanted to stay.
 I don't know how he is now though because he didn't even kiss me good-bye when he ~~just~~ left. I ~~wonder~~ why he didn't, I don't know why, I really don't. Why did he hesitate so much to even leave? He knows that I want a kiss, he knows that I won't ~~p~~ pull away. So what's stopping him?

— Melinda Lyons

The near-death experience diary entry was made sometime after the experience. Please keep in mind, I was still a teenager in school and wasn't in the concern for actual dates at the time of the event. You'll notice I didn't mention my out-of-body experience on the Astral Realm because once I made the motion to block it from memory, I simply forgot it entirely.

What I figured may have happened, is I had undergone a sort of *Selective Amnesia*, which is a type of amnesia in which the victim loses certain parts of their memory due to the trauma.

THE NDE AFTERMATH

For a long while I was constantly sick after my death door experience. It was difficult for my entire family and consumed them with considerable worry, because for a few days after the initial anaphylaxis I would still have hives resurface on my skin. My body was basically still rejecting the amount of beef left in my system and I'd be sleeping all day long from the large amounts of Benadryl I was prescribed once I left the hospital. My mom was checking on me constantly, making sure I was okay nearly every hour. Even my brother Patrick, and little sister Heather would pop their heads in my room every few hours to check in on me. (I have brothers, Pat and Chris that are fraternal twins).

The awesome part was getting less homework because of the over amounts of sympathy from the teachers at my high school. At the time I was taking Japanese language class because I was planning on becoming a Japanese translator, (later I figured out I'd be translating for spirits instead). I took Japanese for four years in high school, and eventually continued it in some universities but learned it wasn't where I belonged. But at the time I was so devoted to learning about the language to teach, help and guide people in a place that was unknown to them.

DO YOU SEE THE PATTERN HERE?...

THE OLD MAN
(FIRST FULL BODIED APPARITION)

What many near-death experiencers may confess are the sudden changes in themselves after the said closeness to death. Not all are expected to be the same and should never be judged nor compared for all are meant to have their own that corresponds with the individual near-death experiencer, with a divine purpose. Though sometimes I admit I wish it were different due to the many frightening things I can experience, but it's ones like this, that remind me of the goodness it can also bring.

Not too long after my hospital visit and upon returning home, I was slowly getting back into the swing of everyday life. Hanging out with friends, eating foods that no longer included beef (took a long time to get used to it) and moving with the motions of school. What I wasn't in the swing of was when I had come face to face with a full-bodied apparition that not only was sitting in our living room but acknowledged my entering the house.

It was on a brightly lit Alaskan summer day where I was coming back into the house through the front door. Not sure why I was coming into the house but knew I was on a mission to either get something or eat something. At the time, the living room and the kitchen weren't separated by a wall, so my parents had placed a couch that was 'L' shaped, to create a wall between the kitchen and the living room. A man happened to be sitting on the couch facing the front door that I entered from. He didn't say anything, but he looked at me with a serenity of peace and didn't speak a word. As I approached him, I initially thought that he must've been one of my parent's friends or co-workers because he wore overalls slightly covering a long-sleeved plaid shirt with a considerable beard. He kind of reminded of my grandpa because he loves plaid and he felt very calm in the area of energy. I never felt any amount of negativity and so to be polite I waved 'hello' at his way while walking by him towards the kitchen. As I did, he gave an equal silent gesture. It wasn't unusual for our house to have new faces because we invited people to our home all the time, but something just didn't seem right, and this feeling came at me immediately after. Once I passed him, that's when I urgently twisted around to find within a matter of seconds the man was now gone. Poof, *vanished!* I still remember rushing to look outside the door, and then to the hallway thinking maybe he went to the bathroom. But nothing. This man disappeared without a trace.

This man never gave off any kind of an eerie vibe, nor did he make any type of signal that he was malevolent. Only, he just seemed odd and that's what ignited my curiosity to look behind me to see if he was still there. But he wasn't. He completely vanished. At that moment I was speechless but not for long, because that's when my mom came into the house and noticed my disturbed expression. And knowing how I've nearly died she's always been the type to comfort all of her five kids. Within seconds my mom asked,

"Honey, what's wrong? Are you okay…?"

It wasn't easy telling my mother this because of all of the times I've tried to tell people about my night light experiences, I figured she would call me crazy too. Not to mention when I first had woken up from my near-death experience in the hospital, I told my mom that I thought I had seen Jesus. Even in this moment she suggested that maybe it was just a possible hallucination from the Benadryl. In that instance, I made the conscious decision to completely shut it off and to never tell a soul again. That was also the day when the memory of my NDE would be completely gone because I shoved it down into my subconscious due to self-doubt.

I don't blame my mom for this at all. It was just how I had reacted and honestly, I feel it was good that I pushed it down. I had too many things in my life that had to be dealt with before I could fully prepare and embrace my awakening process. My mom of course always believed in me as she does now. She's definitely one of my biggest fans and I couldn't have done this too without my mom's guidance and love. She actually helped me later on hearing and connecting with spirit which I found was another one of those bizarre divine alignments.

Back at the edge of still eighteen and nearly died already, I wasn't sure how I was going to tell my mom what I thought I had just encountered. But I knew if I didn't say something, I was always going to feel alone and never really validated that I'm not losing my mind. That's when I finally summed up the courage and told her what just happened…

ME:

"Mom, I think… I just saw a ghost."

The words rolled from my lips with a quiver and a half. I didn't know what the hell I was experiencing but I knew that telling someone would be good for me. When the word 'ghost' reached my mom's ears her expression changed and said, "What do you mean?" After a few minutes of describing the mysterious old man her face and eyes adjusted to a sense of shock and that's when she said,

KATHY (MOM):
"Hold on a minute!" Right then, she bolted to her filing cabinet and pulled out a picture and asked, "Is this the man you saw?"

There in the same picture was the old man with the same white beard, overalls and plaid shirt.

ME:
"That's him! That's who I saw!"

My confirmation ignited a smirk on my mother's witty expression and that's when she said the most chilling conclusion…

KATHY (MOM):
"Honey. This man has been dead for a few years. He used to own the bar down the street, the *Hideaway Bar*."

My mom used to work for a bar and grill down the street from our house at the time and it was called the Hideaway. (Jokingly everyone said it was to hide from their spouse).

Pure excitement was jolting through my body and all I wanted to do was learn more about the paranormal. I couldn't believe that I had encountered a ghost for the first time, and never before did I expect or think that it was just to say hello. What I eventually learned from Yehoshua was the **Ascended Masters** (Higher Benevolent Spirits) asked this man's soul to appear to me so as to be connected with my mom at the bar. It was also here in this paranormal phenomenon that I felt my mom and I got instantly closer from our spiritual experiences. No one else had them like my mom and I did. At least no one else in our family really opened up as comfortable as we were for a long while. She would begin sharing all of her paranormal stories -both funny and scary. The universe gifted me with learning and experiencing my first ghost, but it also gifted my mom and I to open up and get even closer over time. I needed to feel comfortable to talk about it and I learned from hearing about her experiences that she did too.

MELINDA KAY LYONS

THE GOD-FEARING TRAGEDY

Much of today people all over the nation are being heavily triggered by the idea that an angry God judges humanity and places them into a Heaven or a Hell realm for all eternity. This is what troubles Yehoshua and why he asked me to do this. Not because he doesn't want others to still have faith, there's still much room for faith and trust in the benevolent beings on the other side. However, what's got his concern sparked, is the level of fear that's been rising due to the tired ideologies from ancient religions accompanied by the many negative spirits that are endangering humanity. We as a species must continue to reconnect to our energetic roots from where we came from as spiritual beings having a human experience.

The notions that Yehoshua described to me and still communicates with me to this day, is that **LOVE** is all that matters and that the only God we must respect are the ones inside of all of us. Though this seems like a blasphemous statement, allow the words from one of the most famously gossiped lost gospels to entice this conscious advancement. The *Lost Gospel of Thomas* was discovered in Egypt of December 1945 among a group of books known as the *Nag Hammadi Library*. It contains 114 sayings attributed to Jesus that also is worthy to be one of the most important alternative texts. However, it's been declared heresy by the Vatican due to its alternative approach to what it means to find Heaven and God…

DEMON DEALER

"RATHER, THE KINGDOM IS INSIDE OF YOU, AND IT IS OUTSIDE OF YOU. WHEN YOU COME TO KNOW YOURSELVES, THEN YOU WILL BECOME KNOWN, IF YOU DO NOT KNOW YOURSELVES, YOU DWELL IN POVERTY AND IT IS YOU WHO ARE THAT POVERTY."

Such sayings as this point to Gnostic-like ideas, declaring that sonship with God is directly connected to self-understanding and knowledge. In suggested texts like this one in particular, it enables the reader to arrive to a place of limitless possibilities internally. One of the reasons we could assume the Vatican rejected sayings such as this could be due to the fact it rejects the very notion of one's need to be *saved* in order to find Heaven. It signifies that a person doesn't need to attend church, or to abide by all the said Commandments, only to abide by one's internal lessons throughout life and experiences. Each individual is given the power to adhere to their own desires and said motivations or agendas -even the church.

Let's not judge them so harshly for it's common for most that are bred into a religious way of thinking is due to being groomed this way, for no one is meant for strict religious dogma, but are trained. Trained to remain conditioned into the ideology that you do not hold any power of your own and are doomed for all eternity, if you don't abide by those said rules and regulations that many in today's modern society claim is now "love". Ever so loving that the God depicted in the Holy Bible, would kill innocent children, women and men for the sake of all mankind. Let us not be so rude as to neglect the agency that which correlates to all that is Godly. Far too many holy buildings are too interested in reminding you of the many mistakes you've made and how much Hell is only meant for those that do not take full absolute responsibility in said mishaps and faults of their own. Digging into the very conscience of none other than even children so as to catch the grooming method early in hopes they only march along the many others that are too brainwashed.

I was once a heavily devoted Christian with the desire to follow into the idea of pleasing a God -but I did this **purely out of fear**. No one is untouched by the grazing of the cheek with the slap on one side, and the kiss on the other. Speaking from personal internal damnations that I had laid upon my own soulful intended existence. It was only from the many manipulated scriptures that I judged myself so harshly all the way to the point where at the shy age of eight, I believed I somehow deserved my molestation. Only it wasn't until my near-death experience where I was unfolding the cosmic and psychological reality that I too was molested by the mindful tricks from this grooming system. A system that has successfully organized its roots and narrative all over the world, converting even the most educated and naïve of persons.

Once the fire of knowledge ignites within the soul, only then can one truly hold the truth that the only one that is meant to control you -*is you*. You are not meant to be restricted *soulfully* or *psychicly*.

It wasn't until this moment with Yehoshua that I was slowly being introduced into this understanding. However, new knowledge cannot be introduced until the old knowledge is first torn down. Only then can you begin to rebuild where the understanding shall stand while too shaping and designing the structure of your own moral compass. It was here, Yehoshua taught me the divine rule of one's consciousness, that which begins the transcendence into an even deeper spirit evolution and revelation.

Reciting that Yehoshua set our attention on his message that he didn't say all that is quoted by him in the many scriptures. In the *Lost Gospel of Thomas* there was a moment where *Simon Peter* said, *"Make Mary leave us, for females don't deserve life."* In reaction Jesus replies, *"Look, I will guide her to make her male, so that she too may become a living spirit resembling you males. For every female who makes herself male will enter the kingdom of Heaven."*

Now, it's plain to see this not only contradicts the idea of equality that Jesus would emphasize, but it also targets women as an unworthy specimen.

With whole heartedness and respect in the workings of those that believe in the Holy Bible, I must relay with absolute energetic urgency that Yehoshua **didn't** and does **not** support, nor has ever said this type of notion. Women are not only highly respected on the other side, but are viewed and respected as the **DIVINE FEMININE** that are equally worthy to the **DIVINE MASCULINE ENERGY**. And as relayed prior, this would be one of the, oh so many scriptures that are not in alignment with the Yehoshua that many near-death experiencers have encountered.

THE GOD CONSCIOUSNESS

During my near-death experience I did in fact feel as if I were speaking with a bright light that embodied all colors and more than humans could imagine. And although it's divine presence made me feel an immense amounts of security, love, non-judgment and comfort -it was not the God most would assume. After countless experiences from not only benevolent but also malevolent encounters, I've discovered that the Christian God didn't exist. As blunt as this may come across, please understand first and foremost - this was excessively difficult for myself to accept due to my old Christian background. However, over the course of time and from examining all that I've encountered, undergone and experienced it became clearer that there was not a singular God like in the Bible that exists, or to be considered the ultimate source of our existence.

This was not only expressed to me from many other Angels and other spirits, but also from Yehoshua himself. As he sat me down during my astral meeting, he carefully yet flatly revealed to me the *truth*. This trust in yourself may take time to consider for it's not always within the human nature to feel absolute security due to the level of fear that is programed into us since birth. But in his divine dialogue, it was here in this meeting he articulated how each individual person is connected to all the is within the universe and that we are meant to be our own creators of our lives. For we are not limited nor are we meant to be forced into a line of copycats, but instead are light beings fueling with the inner powers of our own levels of creation, healing, guidance and love. We are the masters of our own universe and were meant for something much bigger than what the Christian faith claims.

However, in order for the said souls to be gifted with this awareness, they must first be allowed to be granted permission to let go of the fear of judgment from others. Fear is all too powerful and is as equally enticing as the energy of love. It's not in the nature of humans to be comfortable with taking the reins of their divine power, for we are programmed into the construction of 'follow' and 'obey'. But that's not our purpose in our soulful existence and *it's not yours!* You were meant for a much grander scale of success than what the dogma reveals nor allows you to know. Far too long has humanity been groomed into believing it's a sin to take the compass to your own destiny and allow yourself to be praised for your own good works. It's not evil to congratulate oneself, but then again, we see so many give credit to a God through outside worship to an entity that simply does not exist. Instead, the Godlike being that has always existed is the Godly being inside of you, and in those around you.

Within teachings of Jesus, he too spoke of humans being Gods in the Making, and are to be understood with divine respect that all beings, large or small, all possess a powerful light full of love and creation. Within all of us is a God or Goddess waiting to be unveiled and shaken awake! Each individual life form of the human structure was designed delicately within the universal anatomy to correlate to what it needs in the moment, and what you must become. And it was here, my dear reader, how I eventually learned of the **GOD PARTICLE** that is a part of all of us and is most absolute. Foreign as this may sound, it is what I've been taught and use in my teachings.

The automatic Christian reaction would be that I'm speaking heresy and that it's similar to someone like the antichrist. However, I'm still in full support and belief in the power of love and healing from benevolent spirits from the Heaven realms. This of what I propose isn't meant to initiate an anarchy of spiritualism. Instead is to enlighten one to another level of conscious psychic understanding that you're much more than what the religion allows you to know about yourself. There is nothing wrong in accepting your inner power and harnessing yourself with divine respect, love and understanding.

Guiding that too you're in support of others alike yourself embracing their own Godliness into another realm of their own vibration. None of this suggests that we are a God and should suddenly bring people together similar to a cult like fashion and begin judging and controlling people. *Not even close.* What I bring to the cosmic table is a plate of knowledge and a glass of positive energy that will not only encourage your own growth but give it a *kick start!*

However, as I've stated before I didn't remember this cosmic understanding until eleven years later but when I did, that's when my whole life truly changed.

ELEVEN YEARS LATER

LFM YOUTUBE CHANNEL

When I initially remembered this powerful understanding of our soulful potential, it was nearly exactly 11 years later. The moment the memory began to surface in my mind was nothing short of astounding. For days I had shed tears as pieces of memory would come back to my awareness. There's no simpler way to describe it but that it *shocked* the hell outa me. I just couldn't believe that all of this was arriving in my mind, and so *quickly*. At first, I was beginning to worry that perhaps I was losing my own sanity like many of the haters on my YouTube channel and folks from around the world like to chant. But I knew soulfully this was not only real, but that I was meant to share this information with the rest of the world -*and boy was I not prepared for that.*

I've never been one to be in plays, nor be good at public speaking in front of a live audience. The idea of a lot of people staring at me always gave me anxiety causing me to stutter my words and race my heart. But I knew that I had made a promise to Yehoshua and to the many souls from the other side and to the world, I just didn't know how the hell I was guna deliver it. That's when I decidedly told Yehoshua, aloud…

"Okay… I remember most of it now. As you said I would, -and I still can't believe this is happening right now! But how do I even deliver this? So, for now, I'll do the best I can to listen to see what you say…"

For the rest of my week I'd listen to any messages from spirit that would come to me in myself. It's not customary for folks to initially understand how one hears from spirits, but it's really quite easy once you get the hang of it. All you have to do is basically shut up and listen

-but that was always the hardest part in learning because I'm not good at shutting up.

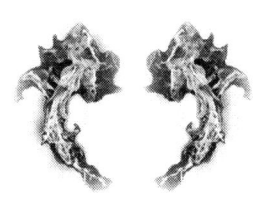

Not to sound cruel, it's just how I simply state it. I'm gentle in my delivery most of the time, but in this book, I wanted to share with you my truest personality as I am. I'm very upfront and pull no punches for it's in my fire sign as a Sagittarius to be outspoken.

It's a way for us to allow the inner voice to begin to tug at our energetic ears to respond to the images, feelings, thoughts and other sensations that will begin to form a full message. Most of the time, the messages from spirits will come all at once like a giant paragraph in an instance. *It's that fast!* Not too long was I forced patience before the word and images of *'YouTube'* kept repeating in my mind. It would arrive similar to like a memory where I was seeing me making a channel and creating a video about my near-death experience. The longer I waited the more nearly irritating it became. Finally, I confessed…

"-Okay, I think you want me to create a YouTube channel? I have no idea on how to do that…unless I ask my brother Christopher…?"

My family and most of those that know my brother are all aware of how freaking talented one of my older brothers is with computers and technology. His intelligence surpasses most of the tech people I've encountered and only trust him when it came to marketing, advertising techniques along with making a website and even a YouTube channel. Not long after speaking with my brother on how to create a channel, I was then also given further advice and many tips on how to build a website and brand myself.

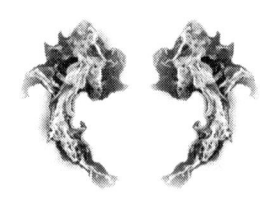

HONESTLY…IF IT WASN'T FOR CHRISTOPHER, I'D NOT BE WHERE I AM TODAY. HIS AMOUNT OF PATIENCE, LOVE AND SMARTASS TOOLS TRULY GAVE ME IMMEASURABLE KNOWLEDGE THAT I'VE USED BECAUSE OF HIM SINCE DAY ONE!

What had gotten me even more amused with how well this divine thing was going, was the fact that eventually a distinct memory surfaced where it was Yehoshua that told me I would be creating a YouTube channel. A guy that wore sandals and lived thousands of years ago somehow knew what YouTube is -but I didn't!? Is there something wrong with this picture?? Many more memories of my soon to be enlightened journey were coming at me nearly all at once. There was not a day where I wasn't receiving more information and the amount of sanity it took to remain aware of myself at all times was struggling, for it would nearly distract me for hours. Over the years I've gotten used to what I call the **PSYCHIC DOWNLOAD.** Humbly I am able to obtain enormous amounts of information from astral experiences and messages from the spirit realm. Sometimes the downloads of information can take up to a few hours, or even a few weeks but a lot of the time it can be as quick as a few seconds to come into my consciousness for me to respond to what I'm receiving.

Once I was able to sum up the guts in starting a new channel, I began making videos but with very little equipment. I didn't have a special video maker except the free one that came with my HP laptop at the time. For Christmas I was gifted a modestly simple camera from my dad that year which helped with that end. But when it came down to anything else like microphones, lights or other kinds of equipment the pro-YouTubers were using, I didn't have any of that nor did I have the amount of money it would take to really get started in a more experienced appearance.

Being a single mother with very little help financially from a certain someone, it became all too overwhelming at first with realizing just how little I had to get it lifted off. So being the person I am, I worked with what I had for lighting which was sunlight in my room and with the idea of just talking to the audience. However, filming those first few videos was horrifying! I would get so nervous to the point where I stumbled my words and my focus so many times that it would take days to film just one video. I'd get over emotional crying for hours feeling like I was going to make an ass of myself (trust me, I definitely did) worried that I was never going to measure up to the other amazingly talented YouTubers. I was comparing myself all the time and when I had first made the channel, I would publish a few videos and then would stop for months and completely forget about it. But when the memory of my near-death experience with Yehoshua came into my awareness, that's when the direction of my channel really started a new transformation.

DUCK HUNTER

People today ask me how I got the courage to start in the first place. But the truth is, I never knew what the hell I was doing, only that I had an important message and that I wanted to make it known to the world somehow. But what a lot of folks don't know is *why* I started the channel. For, I didn't start the channel because of my near-death experience, I started it because I had lost a dear friend whom I loved dearly. Some people have called me crazy and still do, because of my life experience, that even Yehoshua warned me in advanced that most wouldn't take to heart and would harshly judge. That was part of my test in my journey that I knew I had to learn to overcome was the judgments of others that wouldn't understand the slightest idea of just how much I go through within my mediumship and from the mystical moments.

It started when a dear friend of mine, whom I eventually loved and lost. I had met him on a dating website. I had commented on his photos that he looked too good to be on the site to be meeting girls. I honestly didn't think he would respond but within minutes I get a notification on my profile, and to my surprise it said I had gotten a message in response from whom I'll call "Duck Hunter".

We began chatting for a few hours online but then he suggested that we speak on the phone that same night. It's not usual for me to suddenly talk to a person on the phone on the same day we meet on a site like this nor was it for him. He said he would call in about ten minutes and because I didn't have long distance, he had to initiate all of the calls. So nervous at the idea that this amazingly attractive guy even had an interest in talking to me, I checked my hair in the mirror to see if I looked okay, then rolled my eyes at how stupid that was. Nearly at that same time my cell phone rang, and I summed up the courage to pick up the phone and answered to his sweet casual…

DUCK HUNTER:
"Hi…"

Let me sum it up this way by saying, we instantly were *hooked*. We talked on the phone for hours to the point where we later realized it was nearly 5AM that we were still talking. We couldn't stop talking because we would keep discovering how much we had in common.

Though I was a single mom and he didn't have children, what we did have in common was an immense interest in the paranormal. He mentioned he was a part of a paranormal investigation team and was going to locations to try to connect with spirits and hopefully find answers to his many afterlife questions. I hadn't ever been a part of a paranormal team, but I was into learning about it from watching a popular paranormal investigation television show, *Ghost Adventures* hosted by *Zak Bagans*. I only was watching the show at the time, but slowly I started discovering I was predicting things that I couldn't explain, and other situations. I didn't think anything of it, nor did I really take it into consideration that I could be a psychic medium. After mentioning this to "Duck Hunter", he decided for fun that I'd read him. Apprehensively I said…

ME:

"I'm not a psychic, plus I'm sure I'd get a lot of it wrong. I don't even know how to do that kind of thing."

It was here in this moment where he said,

DUCK HUNTER:

"...I don't know how it really works either, but I've met several psychics and they all seem to do it the same sort of way. What I do know is they clear their minds and let the information just come to them gradually. So, just clear your mind and take the first thought that comes to you. Don't worry about being wrong or right, just take what comes to you and go with your gut. And if you're wrong, then no worries."

The way he said this somehow made my nerves all go away in some magical sense. I don't know how or why, but somehow his belief in me made me suddenly feel safe to start believing in myself. When I finally opened myself up, I'll never forget this moment. I was sitting in my computer chair, closed my eyes and breathed in slowly to take in him. I didn't know what I was doing, but I knew that if I wanted to read him, that I'd have to focus my energy on him -on his energy. Once I channeled into him, within a few mere seconds, I got into this **STRONG** energetic pull that felt like I was heavily medicated to calm the nerves. It felt like an energetic cocktail of, 'I don't give a fuck'. I'm sorry, but that's what it felt like. I was suddenly sunken into my chair, feeling as if my arms and legs were numb and heavy and I could barely focus.

He began to get worried for me and asked if I was okay. And it was here in my response where I recited to him what I thought I was seeing and hearing, but these images weren't literal but more of like feelings at the time. It took me a few minutes to finally tell him exactly what I was seeing and sensing because I was too fearful of being wrong. Once I gathered the courage to tell him exactly all that I was sensing, that's when he replied in a yell...

DUCK HUNTER:
"Oh my God, how the hell did you know that?!"

He was beside himself in utter shock saying that he's gone to many psychic mediums and none of them have ever been this accurate before. *Those were his exact words -not mine.* And it was here where he encouraged me to open up to the idea that maybe I should consider taking it seriously as a career. It was also here where he volunteered to help me practice my readings on him and we did. It went on for about a year, both my psychic practice and the building of our friendship.

It's not a surprise that over the course of this time we both developed feelings for one another. His family and friends say otherwise, and they have the right to their opinion with good reasons -but what they don't know is that he called me **regularly**. I never could call him. I could only text him to ask him to call me and so he willingly did whenever I needed it. He was overly supportive and never once made me feel like I'd be terrible as a Psychic Medium.

To be honest, in our friendship, what I miss the most was our late talks on the phone where I'd be sitting on the floor eating cheesecake laughing while he made fun of me. I was my happiest whenever he called or texted. It didn't take long for me to know I loved him. Deep down I just knew he was the one soul I had been waiting my life to meet.

However, in utter humiliation when I expressed how I felt about him, he said we would be better off as friends. Those that knew him physically only know that he denied me, -but what they don't know is he wanted us to be together and I denied him first, and that's what caused him to shut me out romantically.

Though we stayed friends, overtime he then stopped calling as much. When he did call or text, he would ask me to read about a girl he was interested in or dating at the time. It was difficult during these calls, because I'd be sitting on the floor listening as he'd expressed how he was waiting for the right girl, and silently I'd be crying on the other end whispering, *"It's me you idiot..."* But I still wanted him in my life even if I couldn't be with him. I wanted him to be happy even if it meant he was happy with someone else. *That's how much I loved him.*

As the months had passed it was around June, or July that I had a vision while sitting on my bed. I was in the middle of doing something in my room, and then heard a quiet voice tell me to sit on my bed and meditate. Trusting this voice, I listened and did so willingly. I closed my eyes and when I opened them again, I was in a forest surrounded in snow.

This is the part you may have a hard time in believing, but I was actually there! Not like it was in my third eye kind of vision, -no, I was actually physically **THERE!**

One minute I'm in my room in the middle of Alaska summer and then I sit on my bed, close my eyes and **boom**, I'm in the smack of winter walking in a wooded area covered in snow. I could feel the winter chilled air flow into my lungs as I breathed in unsure how I got there. Examining my surroundings not sure of where I was that was when I heard a man yelling for help in the distance. I ran through, passing trees and snow to find a man in what seemed to be a very large pond or lake drowning and crying for help. As I tried to go and reach for him, suddenly I *became* him and was in the water drowning as him. As water was filling into my lungs, the warmth of my body was drastically going cold and no matter how much I tried to reach the surface, I slowly fell below.

But then I was feeling warm again and could see a bright rainbow light hovering over me. Slowly the lids of my eyes closed, I awoke back in my room sitting on my bed, back in the summer heat of Alaska. I gazed at my hands and could still feel the cold air within my whole body. Gasping several times in disbelief of what just happened, it wasn't until a few seconds that I noticed the air escaping my lips was a cold mist.

By November 2012, I was doing dishes by placing silverware in the drawer with the others. Nothing to my mind at the time but that I was simply putting clean dishes away from the dishwasher. It was in a brief moment where I stalled in a calm motionless gesture and said without thinking, "...Duck Hunter's dead." That moment I said it, loads of emotion overcame my mind, body and soul. Tears burst from my eyes as I rushed downstairs to wipe the tears away in fear my daughter may see. But then when I went to the downstairs, I felt a presence in the hall and I could suddenly feel a sense of love, safety, along with smelling a strong aroma of what smelt like Axe which is a brand of a men's cologne. Intuitively I could see in my mind's eye "Duck Hunter" standing in the hallway somehow, and it was here I began crying on the floor while saying…

"You feel like someone I know. You feel like someone I love dearly -and if you're 'Duck Hunter', I'm guna be glad it's you but I'm guna be so fucking pissed!"

Just a few weeks before this happened, I was on the phone with "Duck Hunter" where he said he was going to go on a duck hunting trip with two friends. This trip was something they did every year and have done it since he was a kid, so it wasn't unusual for him to go. I still remember this conversation like it was yesterday. I'll never forget the way he breathed on the other end of the line as he nonchalantly spoke of going to Las Vegas for a trip and that he'd love it if I met him there someday. We even spoke about things in Vegas that I've never seen but all the while during this call as he was talking, I began getting terrible anxiety and a feeling of fear as emotions came over me. That's when he paused asking if I was okay. Hesitant on revealing what I had seen I finally told him…

ME:
"…remember when you said I should go with my first gut on psychic readings…?"

DUCK HUNTER:
"Yeah…?"

ME:
"I have this really bad feeling and I don't know if you should actually go. I keep feeling like something really bad is going to happen."

DUCK HUNTER:

"Well, we are always safe on all of the things we do so I don't see how it could be an issue. We are only going on a lake and…"

ME:

"-A lake? Are you going to wear your life jacket??"

DUCK HUNTER:

"Pff…I'm a fairly good swimmer, I won't need a life jacket. I'll be fine."

Instantly I recited back to him that when you fall into super cold water the muscles in the body lock up and prevent the body from moving and causes the person to drown. However, no matter how many times I tried to persuade him from this reality he kept remaining confident that he would be okay. I even mentioned that the boat could capsize but he laughed it off saying that waves never happen during the winter months on the lake. Though he was well experienced and had done the duck hunting for years it was in my desperation where I then mentioned about the vision I had in my room…

ME:

"…I'm telling you what you told me to do -which is to go with my gut. You always believed in me and in my abilities and I'm asking you to believe me now. I think the vision I had was of you. I don't know how but I feel it deep in my gut that it was a possible warning. You could even make fun of me for the rest of your life over the fact nothing would have happened, but please, *please* wear your life jacket."

But no matter what I said, he wouldn't give in to my plea, so I ended the concern with this…

ME:
"Okay. If you don't want to wear your lifejacket to save your life, - fine. But then you're only thinking about yourself and not the fact you'll be leaving all of your family, friends and those that love you, all because you're too stubborn to wear a life vest. If you die because you didn't listen to what spirit is telling me to warn you about, then at least promise me one thing, -promise you'll at least come back somehow to let me know you're okay and to be my spirit guide."

I wouldn't let him off the phone until he promised. Jokingly he agreed and then we continued our call with a more lighthearted topic but all the while my heart didn't want to get off the phone.

TWIN FLAMES

I thought it was strange that I hadn't heard from "Duck Hunter" in a couple of weeks. When I didn't receive any texts or calls, I decided to check his Facebook. You would've thought that his wall there would've been condolences for the family of the loss, but there was nothing. No sign or indication that something had happened. So, when I messaged his Facebook, I didn't think anything of it. I figured at the most he was busy with life, work or dating another girl that he would eventually ask me about.

But tragically in November 2012 "Duck Hunter" was duck hunting in a boat on a lake but an unexpected wave came causing the boat to capsize. He drowned from not wearing a life jacket.

I had gotten the message from one of his relatives who had let me know on Facebook after they had seen that I wrote him on his wall.

I will never forget this moment. I was in the living room at home one late evening during a cold December night, just a week before my Birthday, I think. When I read the words, "he died". I can't explain anything else but that it was *soulfully excruciating*. My entire body and mind **lost it.** I ran downstairs with my laptop in hand, placed it on my desk and read it again several times out loud. The next few minutes can only be identified as the sound of complete unbearable loss. Like a child, I wept on the floor, sobbing as I screamed in agony as I could only see the same vision I had.

I never knew what it was like to lose someone you desperately loved but when I found out he died, that was the moment I learned this experience deeply. So deep I screamed so loud that my own dad came rushing down to my room to see what was wrong. He came to find me on the floor in my room cowering over my legs as tears streamed down covering my hands. I could barely breathe. I felt like I had lost everything. All of my love I had for him felt like it all died with him. It was also when I realized that it was in fact "Duck Hunter's" soul in my house the entire time since he had crossed over.

I can't fully put into words just how distraught I was over this loss. My soul felt like I had lost my only other half. I felt like I had lost the one person I knew deep inside of all of my being that I wanted to spend the rest of my life with. Without any amount of doubt -I **knew** this absolutely. I've never had that feeling with anyone before, nor since. His energy always made me feel a happiness and I never knew what it felt to be truly in synch with someone -'till he came into my life. And it was from this loss, that I so desperately wanted to open up to the other side as much as humanly possible, as long as that meant I could see or feel him again somehow.

I lost so much of myself when he died. I could barely eat. I would be in my bed for days without eating but maybe a small snack, then I'd be back in bed crying for hours. I'd went down to eighty pounds because of just not wanting to eat. I couldn't even smile, laugh, or had even the slightest interest in spending time with my daughter who was only a toddler at the time. I would just lay in bed sleeping and crying with the shades closed when it was bright and sunny outside. I had no interest in living anymore. It came to the point my twin sister Carolyn, would send me concerned text messages that'd say…

"Minda…you know he wouldn't want you to be this way. You know you should get up and at least eat something…"

I didn't even tell my sister I wasn't eating, but she knew something was wrong when I wouldn't answer her phone calls. This was especially hard for her too because she knew how much he meant to me. She had spoken to him one time on the phone because I wanted her to know what type of guy he was and why I loved him so much.

The hardest lessons I learned from this loss, was that no matter how much you try to deliver a warning from a premonition as a Psychic Medium, it's not your choice in what they do. He had the free will to make the decision to not wear his life vest, and ultimately paid the price. My heart felt utterly responsible and couldn't even open myself for others at the same time, even though I wanted to badly. But I felt this indescribable amount of soul crushing guilt that I didn't do enough to save his life. It felt like I failed him and his family. I truly felt this on every ounce of my being. I felt like I couldn't even trust my own judgement when it came to visions for several years.

After shedding tears of insurmountable odds of this tragic happening, I was given the most beautiful gift which was in seeing him each day since his passing. Even now his soul is with me, knowing how hard this whole journey has been for me and for him. We've been through much hardship and mistakes that even I and him have made. But it's in our forgiveness, love and unbreakable bond that keeps us together regardless of the universal distance between us.

Even typing this for you now, I cannot help but shed tears again. It's hard going back to this place where I once was. Where I felt like he was truly gone forever, but it was from this overpowering urge to connect on every level possible that somehow it opened me up to other aspects of myself psychic-wise. I started to have more dreams, and other kinds of energetic sensations I wasn't aware of feeling before. There would be times where he would awaken me to a dream of hearing his soft voice whisper into my ear and hug me ever so tightly followed with the most tender kiss. Other times I'd be walking in the hallway of the downstairs doing laundry and I'd begin to smell what seemed similar to Axe cologne for men. I'd know this was him because he would follow it with a tender touch on my cheek or something in that compassionate nature.

It wasn't too long when I decided to contact a Psychic hotline to hopefully see if I could make any kind of connection with "Duck Hunter's" soul. The moment I was connected to my chosen Psychic Medium, she was immediately connecting and began to tear up as she felt the sudden pain and the loss I was going through. I didn't tell her much, but the first words she said was, "Honey… are you a widow?" I lost it. I just *lost* it then and there and it was in this first reading experience with this total stranger that she began to confirm all kinds of things for me that there was *no way* she would know.

And it was shortly in this call where she revealed to me that "Duck Hunter" and I have a very unique bond that isn't compared to Soulmates. She told me that we were what's called, **TWIN FLAMES.**

Twin Flames are deeper than the soulmate connection and have a much stronger energetic bond due to being similar to a mirror image of one's energy vibration. Twin Flames are far and few. Souls that are scattered all over the world in the purpose of finding each other to test not only their bond, but their soul purpose for the greater good of all concerned. A journey about love on such a powerful level that is beyond most of the ordinary ideals when it comes to the identification of love and overall relationship goals. It's about discovering your higher self while also looking into your deepest darkest parts to help you grow further through lessons, self-awareness, compassion, forgiveness, mercy and many other things.

The moment she revealed this to me, it suddenly felt like I had finally ***found him***. I don't know how else to describe this, but it felt like I was always on this journey to find someone specifically, and little did I know but that upon discovering and reuniting with him, that my life would ultimately change beyond preparation.

"CRAZY" EXPLAINED

To be truthful, I didn't want to write this portion in my book. I tried this in the past and later learned most of his friends and family would call me crazy and wouldn't like me for being honest about what I experienced and still experience to this day.

I made the mistake of letting people know what I would eventually experience from after he died and of his mistakes. I had made vlogs in hopes that maybe if I told people that possibly experienced the same thing as myself, that it would help me heal or move forward. I said hurtful things and would share what astral experiences he had done that I felt were unloving and unfair. I published quite a few of these vlogs where I openly discussed my pain when he would promise things to me in our Twin Flame bond but then discovered he was being unfaithful and basically cheating on me. (*Yes, you can have a relationship with the departed*) What I didn't know was a few of his friends and family found my videos.

In the beginning for a year where I publicly shared his information, it was all based on positive experiences, so it never seemed to bother them. But once it went to a dark harsh reality of what he had done, that's when I had gotten a backlash.

After I realized how it was causing them to feel, I deleted them in hopes to move on from it. Was this stupid? Yeah. I did it naively not thinking of those that only knew one side of him and it wasn't until they threatened to sue me that I decided to take the videos down. This choice was also when I began having dreams of being sued to the point where I was forced to no longer work as a Psychic Medium and it would ruin my purpose in helping others all over the world. The last thing I wanted to do was ruin my purpose. When I spoke to my mom about it, she told me the dreams were warnings and that it would be wise to take the videos down. I cried on the phone screaming over how unfair the whole situation was. Tears just overflowed onto my desk that I've worked so hard at for basically pennies and hearing that truth of what this could do was extremely difficult.

At first you may be assuming this point of view was selfish of me. One thing most people just don't process is as a Psychic Medium you experience the spirits as if they never died. You know they aren't dead and are just transitioned to another level of existence.

Most Psychic Mediums will never admit to 'normal folk' is that romance between the living and the departed can be very therapeutic for healing, closure and in this case -a lesson learned. What I learned was just because he was given lots of knowledge when you die doesn't suddenly make one wise. Wisdom comes from the many experiences you have and learning from those experiences. The cliché naivety that once a person dies is suddenly one with God or with a higher vibration isn't true in all cases, and I was subjected to learning that my Twin Flame and love of my life, was a lower vibrational soul that hadn't evolved passed certain lessons.

I loved him more than I can express to anyone and even after all of what he's done, I still do. But it didn't matter to anyone living because all they could see was and is a 'crazy obsessed' loser that claims they can talk to spirits and was only trying to hurt his rep, his family and anyone that knew him. But that simply just wasn't the case.

What **SLEEPERS** (*people that haven't awakened*) don't understand is I know the *other side* of him that they don't. When we die, we will do things that we normally wouldn't have done when physically alive because of the amount of immeasurable freedom to do basically whatever we want. Unfortunately, this kind of freedom taken for granted without caution to how it can harm others was his lesson. And it was by losing him that I began to learn this from the many painful experiences that he and I have gone through. What I had to figure out was that not everything is meant to be shared publicly because no matter what, it was only for me and him alone.

In my only defense, the main reason I was posting those vlogs was because I had nothing physical from him to hold on to. I had missed out on meeting my Twin Flame in person -in fact, I was going to surprise him that same year by meeting him on my Birthday on the following December. But when he died, I realized I lost the only chance I had of meeting him.

This isn't an excuse, but it explains *why* I did it. Do I regret vlogging my experiences? No. But do I regret it hurting his family and friends? Yes. I never meant to hurt anyone. My only focus at the time during the vlogging was to document how even your loved ones when they die can change into someone you never thought possible. It wasn't to damage his reputation or to insult the family or those that knew him, but to express the experiences I had and still undergo. I was focused on the exposing the truth about the process of our learning lessons on the other side, but then later realized that his continual betrayals and mistakes would also in-turn become a lesson for myself.

My Twin Flame is an amazingly loving soul that I will never stop loving. The issue is love comes in many shapes and shades and it's not always pretty. No one is perfect and never will I announce to the world or in a room with you that I am either. I make mistakes just like everyone else for my purpose in living was to also learn from my experiences that were also harmful to me and others.

The loss has granted me not only a great tragedy that still aches but has given me the divine ability to connect with someone whom I'm close to. It's not typical for a Medium to be that forward. Most often

I've seen that most Psychic Mediums will keep their deepest darkest secrets to themselves, but now I know why, and it was in sharing too much of a once living person that caused this painful lesson to unfold.

WHY MENTION IT?

I'll never deny my experiences for they are all truthful. Dreading the fact that his soul has caused me much pain since his transition to the other side has nearly exhausted my tolerance for many things. Of course, I wish it wasn't true that he would or could even remotely treat me or anyone the way he did, but it's the truth, nonetheless.

Some may be wondering as to why I've even mentioned this. Some may in fact be thinking it isn't wise to be this honest. But I've decided that if I was going to write a book about me that I was going to be completely transparent in how I came to be. Not exposing all of this would be only suspicious and even look as if I were hiding something -but I have nothing to hide and rather you hear it from the source instead of the countless rumors.

YouTubers have talked about me for several years ever since I started my channel and it got to the point that when the situation broke out, it was like wildfire. I couldn't stop people from talking about it, but I could at least tell the truth and why I did it in the first place. If that's not forthcoming, then I don't know what is.

After that I told myself I would never mention my Twin Flame again. However, overtime it was undeniable that him coming into my life is what started my journey into becoming the Psychic Medium I am now. I wouldn't have gone this far without his love, tears, anger, forgiveness and plenty of other emotions expressed throughout our Astral experiences. And for that, I will always be grateful for his support. By sharing my story and his life, I feel like in a way make amends of the darkened past of us and move forward into wiser, more loving souls. He's forever watching over me, guiding me and being the best Twin Flame I could ask for, and as long as we both admit our faults and express our love for one another…then we are still moving forward positively.

HAUNTED INVITATIONS

INCUBUS

As time progressed, I learned how to meditate and focus on baby steps towards understanding how to ground myself by creating a protective energy barrier, but I confess, I was still very much of a beginner with very little experience.

After "Duck Hunter" and I met I'd start to experience what seemed at first like amazingly lucid wet dreams, but then it would get to the point where I'd wake up from what seemed like a hand pulling on my body, tossing me around and even taking off my underwear. There were several mornings I'd wake up with big blue markings of bruising on my thighs and on my back. Not to mention, I'd discover large amounts of 'aftereffects'. These discoveries were nothing short of alarming and it began to make me highly concerned.

It wasn't long after that I began to look into sexual spirits and the word, "INCUBUS" would pop up all over the internet. The more I read, the more I realized I could be dealing with an actual sexual demon.

I even brought it up to my Twin Flame in one of our phone calls. I can still remember the sound in his voice of worry when he heard about what I was experiencing. He felt helpless, but he tried to calm my nerves by making a joke out of it. After all, I was getting nightly favors by a ghost. How bad could that be?

Fast forward to "Duck Hunter" now being on the other side, and here I am still dealing with the same Incubus. Only little did I know that the same spirit would start to look like my Twin Flame by appearing like him physically, but never did I expect it to get to the level that it did.

There was a night specifically where I clearly recall a horrific scene that has stayed with me. It was so real, so graphic that it had grossly introduced me into the dark side of what spirits can actually do but also force upon you without any amount of struggle. It was my first genuine demonic encounter that made me so distraught that it was also when I began to start developing severe anxiety at night that would develop insomnia where I was too fearful to sleep. It was around 3AM where I was suddenly abruptly awoken to what felt like a man having sex with me in my bed, moving my body rather roughly. It got so physical that it woke me up and I mentioned my Twin Flame's name. But that's when the strong invisible force leaned into my ear and whispered…

"He's not here…"

Instantly in a panic I tried to get up out of this state of consciousness. What I didn't know at the time was I was also on the astral realm. The realm seemed so real to me that I literally thought I was in my bedroom on earth, but instead this demon managed to basically pull me to the astral realm and had me trapped there while he raped me. I then tried to get out of this by asking for my Twin Flame to help me, or Yehoshua, but not a soul came -at least not yet. This took quite a bit of time to get out of, but the entity was pinning me down and eventually pulled my legs up off the astral bed and began dragging me off of my bed. It was a struggle to escape for he was invisible, and I couldn't find a way to counter what it was doing.

That's when I yelled as loud as I could in desperation for **ARCHANGEL MICHAEL** to help me, and it was somehow in this moment where I woke up instantly from the incubus' grasp and was back on earth in my bed.

Being open with spirits and the other side isn't just about opening up with good or loving souls, but you're completely exposing yourself to the rest of what's out there. There isn't a line spirits won't cross and there's no alarm system that's going to give you a heads up sometimes on what's about to happen, and I knew this intuitively. I knew that opening myself up to my Psychic Mediumship abilities fully, was not only going to allow me the opportunity to see benevolent spirits but also the faces of evil.

Maid of Horror

Fast tracking to the following year, I was contacted by some old high school friends. For a large portion of my youth in high school and a few years after that we managed to stay close in our friendship. But after a few years we stopped talking as much, especially after the couple decided to make a life change by moving to Washington. This was good for them and I was genuinely happy that they were able to find a place that gave them more opportunities than they did in Alaska. Though we didn't talk as often, we did try to keep in touch.

When they heard from Carolyn that my Twin Flame had passed away, they decided to reach out to me in hopes that getting me out of Alaska would be therapeutic. They were getting married in a few weeks and had asked me to be their maid of honor and offered to pay for my trip out to their house to stay with them for a few weeks. This was more than an honor to me. I couldn't believe they asked me to be her maid of honor, and it was indeed a beautiful wedding I'll never forget. But I couldn't help but feel this was a chance for me to finally find a break of the pain I was dealing with and hopefully to find some normalcy from the paranormal issues I was having on a nightly basis. So of course, I said yes and was on the plane, while my daughter stayed with my mom and dad for the duration I was gone.

There were moments during my stay that we didn't get along very well, so I would mostly stay to myself in the bedroom they allowed me to sleep in. I wasn't comfortable taking over one of their son's room, but they were insistent and the last thing I wanted was to be rude from their overwhelming amount of generosity.

Being around them day to day allowed me a break from the other side and what was holding me back from living. It was nice for we would hangout watching funny music videos, have a few beers and enjoy our time laughing over the old days as kids. The time of joy and relaxation only lasted for very brief moments however, because I was also battling severe depression.

Never had I ever gone to a doctor to get treated for depression, for I believe much trouble in the mind can be healed through time with yourself in meditation, talks with friends and family, spirit guides and with time away from the world to heal and reflect. Nothing against getting medicine to help you for your own depression, I just never found it to be comfortable for me. I like to try to avoid as much human made medicines if I can to stay open to the spirit realm as much as possible. This is what works for me, and not suggesting that my way of living would work for someone else.

While the visit with their family was helpful, I couldn't help but feel left out and alone. I'd find any excuse to go to the bathroom or bedroom just to cry.

There's an old saying that the first year is the hardest when in mourning, but I knew that I would be shedding these tears for the rest of my life. Over time it's gotten easier, but it's never truly gone.

Even though I knew my Twin Flame and I were just friends, I still felt like I had lost the only person that I would truly ever love again so I'd ask for signs of his presence. One day he gave me a loud confirmation that literally made me jump out of my own way.

For one of the nights, few of the people in the house were going outside to have a cigarette. I'm not a smoker but when I am immensely stressed out, there's times where I'll have a drag. I said I'd be outside to join them but had to get my jacket in the bedroom. I knew instantly in that moment my Twin Flame wasn't happy. The moment I went upstairs, not a minute later when I'm in the hallway by myself, I suddenly heard a very loud, **BANG, BANG** on the bathroom door next to me. It was so loud and unexpected that it caused me to nearly scream. When I realized what happened, I investigated to see if anyone was upstairs awake or in the bathroom. But no one was upstairs and those that were in their rooms were all asleep. Still shaken over this, it only made me want to have a smoke more. He thought that banging the door would make me not want to smoke. He always tried to be a healthy person when alive, and never liked the idea of girls smoking. When I said this to him, I could see a brief image in my head of his frustration laughing over the fact that it only made me want to smoke a cancer stick more.

Though I'm a firm believer in the paranormal and know for a fact that spirits can impact your life on pretty much every level imaginable -I also know that one must first debunk the possible. I'm not saying that I'm a professional Paranormal Investigator, but what I am saying is that whenever a person, a client, or even if I myself experience the paranormal, it's important to test those experiences. Even I will test out the odds by examining how something could possibly be explained. But when I don't find a logical explanation that's when I will rule it paranormal.

DEMON BEGONE!

During my stay with the "couple" and their kids, I not only was still getting confirmations from my Twin Flame, but I began to have nightmares.

These nightmares seemed to happen more after I decided to start meditating for hours. When the couple wouldn't see me for a long period of time, they'd pop their head into the room to check to see if I was alive. Jokingly I'd tell them I was meditating, but the other part was I mostly just wanted to be alone. I would stay in the room meditating for so many hours that I would forget how long I'd be doing it. I'd be meditating at 12PM then check my phone and realize four hours had gone by. But what was happening from this heavy induced spiritual bonding with myself was I began to open my third eye so much that I started having visions nearly every night. These dreams, astral experiences and visions would be really good some nights that I'd be so addicted to it. I honestly just couldn't get enough. Especially if my Twin Flame appeared in dreams for a few nights.

After so many days of repeated meditations, what I didn't realize was that I was allowing myself to be a light so bright due to the drastic surcharge of energy I was vibrating at, that I'd begin to attract negative spirits.

To recall, I had a nightmare that led me down a road into more ideas of exactly what kind of evil lurked behind the astral veil.

Unknowingly I found myself in the house of the couple's home alone, not one family member seemed to be around. I was downstairs in the living room where I heard the male couple's voice coming from his son's bedroom, which was the same room I was sleeping in. When I approached the bedroom, I noticed the hallway was dark and as I inhaled, I could smell a rotten aroma capture my senses.

Upon reaching the door that's when I made sight of the male in the room facing the wall opposite from me. He seemed to be kneeling down on the floor with his head down. He didn't say much, he was quiet. Being a sensitive person, I began to check on him but then abruptly the door to the room slammed shut and locked itself with us inside.

Without delay the walls in the room began to bleed from the roof down to the floor followed with the scent of decay. It was so overpowering it nearly made me want to vomit. As the walls bled you could see every detail as the colors began to pulse with the flow of each drip down on the floor and some even on my shoulders. The walls stole my attention as I was stricken from the sight of what appeared to be breathing walls. The motion could fool even the most skilled of mystics. The sight was **HORRIFYING**.

It's not unusual for demons to come to their victims in this manner, however the amount of effort this entity put forth was extraordinary to say the least. I knew it was a demon for as the walls continued to inhale and exhale, the man then shapeshifted before my very eyes into a gruesome sight. I've never witnessed such a grisly entity before nor was I nearly prepared on how to handle it. My instincts were to run to the door and try to open it, which then humored it. A laughter escaped the demon into the form of sound as he said...

"You can't escape Melinda. You can't escape us. We will always come for you now that you've opened up."

It echoed off the ways of the walls as it too hit into my understanding of the fact this demon somehow knew of my abilities. I never had the intention to see this entity, nor was I taught on what to do if I came into contact with one. But what I did know from much meditation that we all had a power inside of us and that no matter what, you couldn't back down from them or they would win. I just couldn't let that happen. My soul was at stake. This was a ride or die situation and I knew it. Don't ask me how I knew this but somehow deep inside I heard -*face it.*

Seemingly it didn't attack me right away. Instead it spoke from its grotesque trap guided with sharpened teeth. Mainly it seemed to guard the door and wouldn't let me through and proceeded to call itself by several names. Not aware of it's abilities, it didn't take long for me to begin prayer for an Angel's help from the decaying cage I was trapped in, but again the demon shunned with the same sarcasm.

DEMON:
"THEY CAN'T HEAR YOU MELINDA. THEY WON'T COME FOR YOU FOR WE ARE ALL TOO POWERFUL."

ME:
"What do you mean *we*? There's only you."

DEMON:
"YOU HUMANS DON'T KNOW ANYTHING... WE ARE AN ARMY OF THE ALL-POWERFUL DARK LORD."

ME:
"You mean *Satan?*"

DEMON:
"MY LORD HAS MANY NAMES BUT THAT IS ONE YOU MAY CALL HIS MAJESTY."

ME:
"He is no lord nor a name to be respected. God is the Almighty Lord, *not* Satan."

(keep in mind this was before I fully remembered my near-death experience and of our God Particle).

DEMON:
"DON'T YOU INSULT MY MASTER! HE IS FAR MORE POWERFUL THAN YOUR FAKE GOD! HE IS THE ONE THAT SURPASSES ALL THAT EXISTS AND CAN TAKE DOWN ANYONE IN HIS WAY. EVEN YOU!"

ME:
"…Why are you here? What do you want?"

In this question the malevolent spirit smiled wide showing the pride and scheme in his eyes…

DEMON:
"YOU ARE SOMEONE HE WANTS. YOU DON'T EVEN KNOW WHAT OR WHO YOU ARE, BUT MY LORD DOES, AND HE INSTRUCTED I STOP YOU BEFORE YOU FIND OUT."

The puzzle didn't stand out to me on just what the demon was referring to, but it did lead me to question this…

ME:
"Why would Satan be so focused on me? -Unless it's something about me he's afraid of…? Doesn't sound like a tough lord if he's so fearful of me."

It was here I began to ponder in on what the demon wasn't saying outright but it suggested that this demon was purposefully demanded to confront me for a reason. A big reason that I still had no idea about.

DEMON:
"HE ISN'T AFRAID OF YOU AND NEITHER AM I!"

With that, the obeying creature lunged at me with full force throwing us both against the wall opposite the door. Both of our bodies flung crashing in the contact of the breathing wall. The smell engrossed us as I was now pinned against my will unable to move. Sinking it's nose into my neck as it inhaled the smell of my fear snarling as I visually noticed it's pleasure in my uncertainty.

DEMON:
"CAN YOU SMELL THAT? YOUR FEAR...? IT'S SSSOOOO... TANTALIZING."

A long slimy tongue slithered up the left side of my neck as perversion smeared against my skin. Isolating fear took hold of my ability to do anything, I was without hope that is until a female voice called to me...

FEMALE VOICE:

"Melinda, you aren't alone. You must fight it back! You can do this!"

Apprehensive I thought, *'I can't!'*, but somehow the voice could hear my thoughts and said…

FEMALE VOICE:

"-Yes, you can! You have a powerful light inside of you! Don't be afraid Melinda, use all of your soul might to fight it! We believe in you! Melinda - **GET MAD!**"

I'm not exactly sure if it was my soul that decided this or if it was because I felt like I had permission from an unknown voice to fight back, but mysteriously a power came over me. A sense like a supernatural ability to confront this evildoer guided by an absolute focus in knowing exactly what to do. A lifeline of strategic battle tact escaped me as I managed to maneuver my body from the wall and the demon, giving me the chance to run towards the door for a second try. But it wasn't long before the demon yanked my hair and slammed me down on the floor in the middle of the room and jumped on top of me. The weight of the obedient beast gave it too much leverage which prevented me from escaping. That moment a bright light manifested out of what seemed like nowhere and smashed into the demon's back throwing him off of me.

I assumed this was the help of the mysterious female voice and in that same instance the door opened. That was when I *bolted*. Running out of the room as fast as I could, but then I stopped as I noticed there was a window in the hallway. This window isn't originally in the hallway of their home, so I knew that the entire location of where I was somehow changed. When I spotted the window, I had an idea in my mind as quick as I saw the tiny bit of light gleaming from a tiny crack in the window. That's when I did probably the dumbest thing I could've done. I taunted it.

ME:
"Hey, what's your master guna think when he knows I got away? - Come at me fucker!"

A powerful sound came from the son's room as the demon yelled in reaction. Following after me it scrambled out from the door charging at me at full speed. Not sure how I was going to do this I readied myself by holding my footing as we both collided in the darkened hallway where neither friend nor foe could predict what happened next. Struggling to overcome the beatings the demon lashed against me, in some level of confidence I managed to grapple his back now taking over his ability to hit me. Scared of how this could go, I knew that if I didn't act fast my opportunity might be lost and it could go worse than I thought. And that's when I decided to make our way toward the gleam of light by shimmying it to the window. Using all my might I lunged my entire weight of thought with body flow towards the window that easily could've been believed as an ordered attack. Both of us tumbled in the darkness to the floor of the hall, suddenly rolling towards the light. Forgetting I was in full battle with a demonic entity that could call on other minions at any time, my sight was on that window of hope. Anger surging every inch of me and with much struggle against the mighty foe and after several failed attempts, I was now pinned on the floor of the hall. My back to the floor unable to move as the demon topped over me now with an even more pissed off view of my humanity. Finding satisfaction over its second victory it lingered in a glare while saying…

DEMON:
"SEE…YOU WILL NEVER WIN. YOU HAVE NO POWER OVER US. YOU'RE ALONE MELINDA. NO ONE AND NOTHING IS GOING TO STOP US."

ME:
"I'm not trying to stop you, but I am trying to get the hell away from you. And I'm not alone."

Demon:
"If you're not alone, then where is your help?! There is no one coming to save you!"

As those words flared from the view of hate, I thought that maybe it was right. A sadness came into me that pounded onto my heart of conscience wondering why the female voice wouldn't just come to my rescue. But as the thought waved over me, a rejuvenated universal alliance of truth manifested into my awareness. What came from my mouth in response can only be described as a revelation that I knew I was being tested...

My Higher Self:
"It is not in the battle that makes one tough,
but in the heart of how one overcomes what is rough.

One can only go so far in hate and despair,
For its within ones love, courage and sacrifice that can relieve one from fear."

And it's in this moment I picked up rubble from the debris of our astral battle that was next to me and threw it in the direction of the window. As ambitious my attempt was, the demon jumped to catch the rock preventing it from crashing into the source of deliverance. Tired of this game of sheep and wolf, I hurled myself on top of him again, gripping my fingers into it's ears. In reaction the demon slashed at my face but already prepared, used my body weight to throw him down to the ground slamming his face to the floor. This time I had reins to the role and that's when my foot met the window in a shrieking clash. Glass flew in every direction as the demon screamed in anguish. A supreme bright light flooded the hall and the demon disintegrated into particles floating into nothingness. The demon I was facing in my friend's home was now fading into the abys of glimmer.

I didn't know I was going to be working as a Demonologist at the time, but upon waking up from my unexpected astral nightmare -I knew that what the demon said was going to stick with me for the rest of the trip.

Holocaust Demon

During the time of my visit in Washington for my friend's wedding, I was also invited by another dear friend Kristian, who happened to be living in Portland, Oregon. We both exchanged phone numbers after talking on Facebook. He and my twin sister used to roommate together a few years back when she was attending a university in his city at the time. When he heard I was finally somewhere close enough, drove all the way to my friend's house and surprised me. I couldn't believe he actually drove nearly six hours to come and pick me up just to visit him for a week. Excitedly of course I quickly packed my bags and threw my stuff in his car and we headed off to another adventure.

So much love and care we shared on this trip. He truly is one of the nicest people I know. Though Kristian is a devoted Christian, he never once judged me on my abilities as a Medium nor is he ever afraid to be an ear to listen about the paranormal experiences I was having. On our drive to Portland, Oregon we would talk and laugh about how our lives have been and he was able to be the support I needed after all of the saddened reminder of the loss of my friend.

When we arrived in Portland, I remember feeling a large sense of energy that I wasn't so aware of at the time, but felt it wasn't good. There's an old saying that the larger the city and the more crime in the area, the more negativity in the energy and in the people. This was especially the case the moment I arrived. The city is beautiful with its own cultural nature that I much admired and appreciated, but I couldn't help but notice the negative vibration I was receiving the entire time I was in Portland. Honestly, it almost felt like I had just drove into a massive cloud of negative energy that felt like it was mucky or dirty. It just didn't feel positive to me even though my mindset was positive during the entire visit.

Passing the apartment buildings and bridges, I could clearly recall how many of the homes were old and I could sense that nearly most of these homes more than likely had much residual energy with a spirit or two wandering about. Being so distracted in my thoughts, I soon realized Kristian had parked by his apartment and we had finally arrived.

As I walked out of the car, I felt the breeze on my face, then drifted my eyes to what appeared to be a considerably tired looking building. The brick that helped create the body of the many homes for others in the city seemed to have a story of their own and I knew that this building had suffered many experiences.

With little effort I looked up to the sky as I gazed higher to the top and asked Kristian…

ME:
"Hey, I know this is going to sound random and maybe a bit strange, but I keep seeing the Titanic when I look at this building. Do you know when this building was built?"

He looked at me entertained by the idea and replied…

KRISTIAN:
"I don't know, but that's a good question. -I do know it was built a long time ago."

And that was it about the building and we took my belongings and hustled up the several flights of stairs after entering through the heavy door. I can still remember the smell of the whole space being like mold. Sometimes the whole hall would smell of really bad food someone had made in their apartment down a ways, but sometimes you'd get the smell of cleaning solution from a janitor mopping the floor. It wasn't tantalizing and it nearly made me sick.

Strolling into his apartment I couldn't help but notice the small space. Luckily, he had good taste, so it felt like a small home for someone to feel comfortable for long periods of time. However, the welcome feeling was overtaken the moment I looked to my right and noticed a brick wall that was different from all of the other walls. Throughout his entire apartment was normal white walls, but this wall was the only one with the same brick that was used from the exterior of the building. I quickly became like a moth to a light and walked to the wall and just had to touch it. The texture of the brick meeting the tips of my fingers as I slid them up, and then in a circular motion to the left and then to my right was all very intimate. The energy in the brick felt like I was meeting history for the first time and the brick was introducing itself to me. I couldn't help myself. The sensations of the vibrations felt like home somehow and took time to introduce myself to what felt like a piece of memory.

Don't get this confused. This wasn't a good feeling for it was more like sadness or a harsh time that couldn't be shaken off. Not even the strongest earthquake could shake away the energetic debris the brick held inside. For some mysterious reason I felt sad when I saw the brick, and when I engaged with it. If walls could talk, this brick wall definitely would be one I'd go to first!

During my stay with Kristian I would stay at his apartment most of the day while he was busy with work. To be honest, I can't remember if he was attending school at this time -I think he was but I do know for sure that he was gone most of the day, so I stayed there alone a lot. Staying in Kristian's apartment was admittedly boring, but I was able to catch up on meditation, searching the internet for more articles on learning about the paranormal and keeping in touch with family on social media. During the day it wasn't so bad, but to say it was all good, would be a lie. It still didn't feel right.

Most of the time I felt like I was being heavily observed from someone else in the room. Though no other person was physically with me, I'd still sense a presence in the apartment that was eerie enough that I'd have goosebumps appear on my arms and legs. It was especially uncomfortable when bathing. The moment I'd begin to undress to change my clothes, go to the bathroom, or anything to do with my body felt like I was being visually violated. I didn't know how to handle this, and I certainly didn't want to tell Kristian and cause him to feel guilty for having to work. Decidedly I kept it to myself as long as I could, but it started to get much worse awfully quickly.

DEMON DEALER

When it came to sleeping arrangements, Kristian didn't have a spare bed, so we shared his futon like two mature adults. Although we only known each other a little while and this was our first time being physically together as friends -oddly it didn't bother me. Plus knowing my sister Carolyn vouched on his ability of being a respectable person eased my comfortability. The moment I first saw Kristian at my friend's house was an instant positive vibe that I don't get from folks often. I knew I had nothing to worry about when it came to my safety or any means of concern. In fact, it was a fun time sleeping in the same bed with Kristian, because we would stay up late talking about the idea of God, The Holy Bible and about our own paranormal experiences. We would even spend nights vegging out on junk food while watching funny movies on his TV after he connected it to YouTube and laugh from nonstop standup comedies. I'm a sucker for jokes and junk food.

I only stayed with Kristian for about a week, but regrettably that entire week would become one of my haunting experiences. At first it would be like someone was putting their face up super close to mine at the edge of the futon. Kristian would sleep against the wall while I was on the outside of the bed. Each time I'd lay down to sleep I would have to put my arm over my head or turn facing the wall because I kept feeling as if someone was starting at me intensely. It would get to the point I'd feel breath reach my cheek followed by a growl in the hallway. I didn't know if this was just my paranoia, so

I'd shrug it off but then the next night I'd begin to feel a tug on my leg as if someone was pulling me out of bed. These tugs were extremely hard too. I'd wake up several times per night in utter fear from feeling the tug of a full hand on my leg. I'd wake up with bruises on my legs that were so big that it even led Kristian to worry. On the third night I began to have nightmares so scary that I'd wake up frightened. And each time I would check to see the time it would be around 3AM. I started to panic at this point. I wasn't sure what I was dealing with, but I feared it more than likely could've been another evil spirit that wasn't happy I was there.

The following morning Kristian went back to work and I stayed in the apartment. The emotions of depression and grief would consume my thoughts so much that I'd be crying for hours from the loss of my Twin Flame.

I'd eventually read that his friends and family were calling me crazy on his personal Facebook page, after I made some comments on my spiritual experiences and how grateful I was for his love and guidance. But they hated me from the moment I began to be open in the public about my experiences and was so hurt by this negative backlash that I started having panic attacks.
(Their hate happened before I started YouTube. They hated me that quick).

Their excessive lashing of "…You're not psychic -more like psycho." would swirl in my head like an angry tornado. But then that same night later, I dreamed of my Twin Flame talking with me in the bathroom telling me that he was sorry about what his friends were saying while reassuring me I wasn't crazy.

His hands in mine would be so warm that I could feel the love in the whole space. However, it didn't take long for his smile to fade and a serious look took over and that's when he said…

TWIN FLAME:
"Melinda there's something you need to know though. I'm here because there's a really bad spirit here and he's pissed off that you're in the apartment. He doesn't like women and I'm really scared he's going to try to hurt you."

He was so concerned for my safety and said he was going to do the best he could to stay, though he didn't want to be in the apartment because this negatively charged entity was so gruesome, that it made him **VERY** uncomfortable. I remember that I then reminded him that if anything happened, to seek help from Angels. What struck me in confusion is remembering that he said he had never seen an Angel yet but promised that he was going to seek help from one if he could.

That next morning after Kristian left for work, I decided to directly talk to the entity. As frightened as it made me feel, I knew I didn't have much of a choice. Most would say this isn't a good idea, but I highly believe that you can't deal with bullies without giving them a piece of your mindset on what your boundaries are and what you will or won't tolerate. Entities like this are what I consider astral bullies. They like to take it upon themselves to attack the living and the dead for personal energetic gain.

However, I didn't realize, I was going to eventually learn exactly how they can attack. But talking to the spirit felt like I could also show it I was aware of its presence and that I didn't want trouble, which is actually what I told it. But apparently it didn't do any good -in fact I think it made it even more mad.

This next portion might as well be a turning point to the level of malevolence that not even I think the most trained of Demonologists could've prepared for. This experience was so graphic and daunting that it still stains my memory to this very day as I write this for you. In fact, I had to personally speak with my spirit guides who are, respectful **ASCENDED MASTERS** that are specifically trained for this sort of thing, to make sure this entity didn't come back to haunt me when writing this.

What I didn't know was the entity in the apartment had been haunting the building for a very long time. I'm honestly not sure exactly how long, but I definitely am certain that this spirit loves the taste of **BLOOD**, **HATE**, **PAIN** and anything relating to the vibration of **DIABOLICAL**.

On the fourth night I knew something wasn't right. And my instincts were spot on due to the instance my eyes closed to sleep, as

I caught the sight of a dark shadowy figure that swarmed over, climbed itself on top of me and began to choke me. What I wasn't aware of at the time was I started to see the spirit through my third eye, which can be visually lucid the moment one falls asleep.

I scrambled to get free but it's grip was so tight that I couldn't seem to do anything, not even scream. I then saw his face and he appeared as a Caucasian male with blonde hair, but his facial features along with his eyes didn't seem human to me. His eyes were red and pulsating so violently that you could make out the jolts in his stare the moment his eyes met with mine. I don't recall much except that he began to hit me in the face, punching and slapping me while telling me to leave. Shouting…

"You stupid cunt! Get the fuck out of my space! You and the rest of the bitches disgust me you ugly slut!"

Each blow to my face, **HURT**. Each strike felt like a burn to my skin. Tears erupted from my eyes for I didn't know what I was going to do but tried my hardest to fight back. I didn't know where my Twin Flame was but knew that I had to get him OFF. It was so violent the way he hit me. His weight on my waist felt so real, I truly felt like I was suddenly kidnapped in a dream and couldn't get out. I begged him to let me go and that I'd leave as soon as I woke up. But instead the blonde bully started to choke me with his bare astral hands and that's when I began calling onto God, but the entity just laughed like the last one.

In sheer desperation I shouted for Jesus and I immediately woke up to myself coughing loud and hard gasping for air. I was so loud even Kristian woke up and asked what had happened. I tried to describe the experience to him but I was fearful he would think I was crazy so I only told him that I had a bad dream and couldn't breathe. It was exceedingly difficult to go back to sleep but when I did, that's when it got **MUCH WORSE**.

This entity was draining my energy so much that I could barely stay awake most days without having cat naps that would turn into three hours. And no matter how short lived these naps were, they were always horrible nightmares. Truth be told the daylight didn't take away the darkness in my mind nor would it prevent the sun from going down in the evening. These nightmares were so constant that I started to refuse to sleep as long as I possibly could.

What happened on one of the few nights I slept in that building is one of the hardest experiences I've ever gone through. All jokes aside, this experience shook my entire energy inside of me. It awakened me to a world so malevolent that I feared ever sleeping again.

Eventually after much fighting the sleep tug, I knew the entity was still in the building, still staring at me in a corner just waiting patiently for my consciousness to shift to the astral world. And when I did, I suddenly found my body in bed lying next to Kristian, but then a dark shadow figure grabbed my legs and pulled me out of the bed and began dragging me towards the main door of the apartment. The astral realm felt so real to me, I could grab onto the bed, the floor and even tried to call out to Kristian but he didn't hear me and my strength to gain control of the situation wasn't doing any good. And no matter how many times I cried out to Kristian, he laid asleep as if not hearing a sound. No matter how much I tried to hold onto the door frame, the entity was stronger, and ruthlessly yanked me out of the door with it slamming shut behind me.

The next moment I remember is finding myself being pulled into darkness. As if suddenly I was teleported from one location to another. Within seconds I was engulfed in a black hole and then I was unexpectedly in a place of sunshine beauty at an unknown location.

I didn't know where I was. Nothing in this place seemed familiar. Only thing I knew was that I was now at a location that I didn't initiate myself and didn't know how to get back to Kristian's apartment. Pondering the thoughts while examining the premises, I noticed there was a large building that looked similar to like a factory or a giant house. The roof came to a point towards the clouds, some of the windows seemed broken into and no one seemed to be in sight - except for one woman. As I laid my gaze on her I realized in her eyes she had immense amount of fear, fear that I couldn't relate to nor that

I could comprehend. And that's when she came running to me in tears pleading…

"PLEASE HELP ME! DON'T LET THEM TAKE ME!!"

I was frightened! I had no idea where I was, who she was or what she wanted. That's when I asked…

ME:
"What -help you how? -Who's taking you??!!"

But it was then a group of men took the defenseless woman that pleaded for her life. They didn't flinch nor care that she was in tears crying for mercy. All she wanted was to be free and to go home to those she loved and whoever loved her. But they didn't care. All they did was drag her by the arms towards the building. But what got me the most was the group of men that took her, then turned around and grabbed me and began dragging me to the same fate.

Equally pleading for mercy from the same careless men that I then realized were all wearing the same uniforms. Peering at the badges that wrapped around their arms, that's when I began to panic when I recognized the symbol all too well. I was now in custody of Nazi German soldiers. I kicked and screamed trying every measure I could to get away from them, but nothing seemed to work. In an effort to escape I attempted to bite one of the soldiers but then they slammed me in the face causing my body to fall to the dusty gravel. As I opened my eyes trying to overcome the searing pain now overtaking my head, I then heard a familiar voice that was echoing over me. Looking at the boots that stood in front of me and following the sight to the owner's face, I then saw the same blonde haired, blue eyed man that was from Kristian's apartment.

Crying from the pain and the confusion, I pleaded again to be freed, but he only chuckled at me with a sickening pleasure that aroused over his face. He liked this -he liked pain. They all did. And that's when he said…

Nazi Demon:
"You and her, are an abomination, and neither need to exist anymore."

Barely able to see because of the pain taking over my concentration, I struggled but summed up the ability to reply…

Me:
"You're Nazis. I get it. -But how could you do this to people?? To this woman?? She's done nothing to you, and neither have I! -Plus, I'm not a Jew, I'm German! Isn't that against your code to Hitler?!"

I didn't understand what or why this was happening to me, but I wanted to. I then asked...

ME:
"What do you want? Why are you doing this to me?? I haven't done anything to you! Why can't you just leave us alone?!"

The murderous blonde laughed as he answered...

NAZI DEMON:
"BECAUSE YOU HAVE TO KNOW YOUR PLACE AND WHERE YOU BELONG. YOU HAVE NO POWER OVER ME OR ANY OF US. YOU'RE JUST A STUPID LITTLE GIRL WITH VERY LITTLE. A SLUT THAT ONLY NEEDS TO OPEN HER LEGS AND KEEP HER FILTHY MOUTH SHUT."

What hasn't been told yet, is that during my stay in Kristian's apartment I'd have dreams where I thought I was making love to a beautiful blonde man that cared for me. But the more times I'd have these dreams the more violent he became to the point he would start raping me each time I laid down to sleep. It became so painful I'd wake up hurting from my thighs having severe bruising. I felt so embarrassed and even ashamed thinking that even a spirit would care for me at all. It was personal, it was powerful, and I wanted to believe maybe this entity cared for me, but it only became evident he didn't care about me at all. He used me, and then shamed me for what he wanted in the first place. (Not the first man to do this to me. It takes two to tango).

The view of the men came to me at a halt when I captured the pulsating eyes staring down at me. Each had some form of secret identity I didn't quite get at the time, but I could sense that each person didn't feel quite human, none of them did. Not even the blonde man.

The talking was over and that's when he dragged me by the hair towards the building. I remember the gavel under my feet cutting them as I tried to pull away as hard as I possibly could, but nothing seemed to work. Only that my next moment would become one that would haunt me for the rest of my life.

As strange as this sounds, I suddenly blacked out and then found myself in a room that was dark with a giant glass window that separated me from another room. In the darkened room I saw the same woman, but she was now being strapped into a hospital bed that was up in a seating position. She begged the same men to let her go but they didn't listen, none of them even flinched or looked at her. It was as if she wasn't even there, all they did was strap her in the bed, locking her in place so she couldn't move her arms and legs. When they finished fastening the leather straps, they walked out of the room and locked the door. One of the men was now wearing what appeared to be a white doctor coat and a mask with black gloves. As the men spoke in German, they acknowledged the importance of remaining a certain distance and most of them walked out of the building entirely. But not the blonde Nazi, he proceeded to stay and watch with a smirk.

    Still in the room with the woman strapped in the bed, I then suddenly noticed my vision began to morph into a kind of Godlike sight. I could see the details of everything possible. I could make out the moldy roof, the holes in the walls and the scars followed by the fear on the woman's face. For what the doctor did, was attach her to a kind of chemical that hung next to her in a clear bag that was going to be injected into her arm. The sight of her panic was unbearable. As I lingered my view towards her that's when she suddenly turned her head to me as tears ran down her swollen cheeks. Sheer terror crushed any amount of hope as slowly she pleaded, *"Help...me..."* -and the next thing I remember was witnessing her boil with blisters developing all over her face and body. Painfully they grew larger to the point where she screamed in agony as the blisters began to enlarge tearing open her skin allowing blood and the chemical to seep out of her pores that was injected into her system. Following her screams, was a green smoke emerging into the room flooding the area with a rotten smell that made it difficult for me to breathe. Something in this smoke is what then made her body blister so rapidly that the last thing I captured was her whole body exploding in blood, puss and every possible organ you can imagine. Her whole body just fucking exploded everywhere, and even parts of her flew onto me.

I was so overwhelmed with fear and panic that I couldn't help but scream uncontrollably. And without hesitation, that's when the same men from the other side of the window unlocked the door, and then proceeded to place me into the same seat. Fear cannot be expressed in this moment. All I can say is my fear was so overwhelming that I screamed as loud as I could begging for Jesus or Archangel Michael to save me and then that's when I woke up back in Kristian's apartment for what seemed way too many times.

DURING THE TIME OF MY STAY, KRISTIAN HAD GOOGLED THE YEAR HIS APARTMENT BUILDING WAS BUILT. IT WAS BUILT IN 1912...
THE SAME YEAR THE TITANIC SANK.

Hellish Relations

Dating Deal Breaker

One time I had a psychic reading from a fellow Psychic Medium whom I thought would maybe give me some positive advice or premonition of my life in the future. I was desperate for answers after my trip, and after my awakening to my abilities, and knew I needed some clear insight of where my life would be headed or what would come of my future.

Though I'm not one for future readings, sometimes they're okay as long as you're asking for questions that are based on the heart, not one's ego. This can be seen as me being a hypocrite because I refuse to do future based readings for clients. I have done them for clients in the past and still do at times, but make sure that clients understand it's only done when it's absolutely necessary in order to alleviate concerns or worry for the person and others involved for the greater good. There's a right and a wrong way in doing future based readings, because let's be real,

ANYONE CAN MAKE SHIT UP

Anyone can say whatever you want to hear to make you feel better about yourself, but there's only a small few of genuine authentic Psychic Mediums out there like myself, that will give it to you straight and be real with what you need to hear, not what you want to hear. And that's also why I stopped doing them. I started learning how upset people would get when they didn't get the answers they wanted or expected and then would accuse me of being a con artist just because I didn't give them what they wanted. But that's not how psychic readings work. We don't always get what we want in life and neither do we in a reading.

And during this reading unfortunately, I too was reminded how my own psychic premonitions weren't going to be the best. I'll never forget the moment when I first spoke to this woman. I can't recall exactly how I discovered her, but I know it had something to do with a psychic website that featured her, and contact information. When we got to talking, she immediately picked up on my energy and I never told this woman anything and she started picking up all kinds of things. But what got to me so deep was she then said, "You're single, right?" I breathed and said…

ME:
"Yes."

Then she paused and said, "…And you opened up to your abilities and you're not married, and you're single with a child…?"

I then answered again with another…

ME:
"Yes. Why?"

Without hesitation she answered, "Well, dear be prepared to be single for most of your life…"

To be honest, this still haunts me. What she said hit me like a ton of bricks. Deep down I always knew I'd be single for a long while, but I never thought that it could go to the lengths of most of my damn life. It hurt deep. It truly did. I would cry about this all the time. And the worst part about it was the older I got and the more advanced and experienced I became in my work professionally, the more I learned she might have been right.

What a lot of people don't get is once you awaken to your abilities psychicly, you no longer see relationships the same way ever again. You don't look at love the same way again, nor do you hold people to the same expectations or standards like you probably once did before awakening. Relationships, sex, love and dating in general become something more like a bonding experience where you want to embrace moments, -not conditions, conveniences or shallow expectations.

Don't get me wrong. There have been plenty of eligible bachelors that ask me out on dates either on social media, in person or in other forms of contact. But most of the time they are based on convenience. When I was in my twenties, I used to date anyone that basically I liked and whether or not we were both available for each other. Maybe it's because I'm older now, but even then, when I had my daughter in my early twenties, I knew I wanted an honest, loyal and committed relationship that would lead to marriage, but none of the men I dated were serious about me. They only dated me for one thing, and it *wasn't* because of my mind. Granted there's been maybe only two past relationships I had that were semi-serious but none to the point where they really put in the effort that I did. That's me being honest.

Now however, when I think about dating at all my whole focus is on whether or not me and the other person click energetically. Whether or not he and I resonate on a cosmic level and will truly vibrate on a soul radiance in order to continue to expand growth of our souls. Each relationship is a soul vibrational pull, and with that pull we become attracted to other people for specific energetic reasons based on our souls vibrating on a specific level of desires, understandings and ultimate goals. The only downfall is even though I am attracting plenty of available men, doesn't mean they want to date me for the reasons they think.

ENERGY RELATIONS

It's not so shocking when we observe how a couple that seemed to be going so well suddenly breakup unexpectedly. However, the reason we breakup is actually because of one of the many possible energy reasons:

A) BECAUSE A PARTNER CHEATED AND IS FOCUSED ON EGO.

B) A PARTNER DRIFTED AWAY AND JUST LOST INTEREST IN THE OTHER.
C) BOTH PARTNERS DECIDED THEY DIDN'T MESH WELL AND AGREED TO SPLIT.
D) THE RELATIONSHIP BECAME VIOLENTLY TOXIC INVOLVING ABUSE, DRUGS AND OR ALCOHOL.
E) OR... BECAUSE ONE OF THE PARTNERS DIED AND HAD TO MOVE FORWARD.

Of course, there's many other reasons why people breakup, but these are the most common of causes. Regardless, the split of two partners is due to the energy in one or both partners no longer resonating together. Once the souls vibrations no longer harmonize, they drift to find another energy that matches their vibration. Each soul has what's identified as a **SOUL DNA**, and this is a vibration of energy that we all possess that allows the soul to vibrate at its own pace no matter what is around them. We all have our own vibration that is different from another, but when we do come into contact with another that happens to vibrate at the same frequency, it may feel like you've met a likeness that seems close to intoxicating. You get nothing but the best possible vibe from this person and you want to be around them all the time because you both just *get* each other. This is called a **SOUL RESONANCE**. This is a beautiful moment because it allows both souls to harmonize and explore one another without judgment and pursue each other without apologies in a loving way. It'll be so grand, it'll be as if time had stopped even though you've been in each other's company for hours of the day and it only felt like a few minutes. With this resonance, the souls are able to build each other to their next level of ascension soulfully.

I don't want to get lost here because I know this may seem off the topic of this book, but the reason why I've brought this up is due to the exact reason why dating for me **SUCKS**.

The point is, each person I dated I've discovered that they were all for learning experiences and nothing to do with love. Each time I dated someone I'd find I needed to heal them in some way or because it was a lesson of some kind. The worst part about each one of them is no matter how much I cared about these men, they all seemed to still only care about themselves and never took the time to consider how I really felt. Nearly all of them were like this. The more I grew within self-awareness vibrationally, soulfully and psychically, the more I began to learn that most of the men I dated never actually loved me, but were only with me for lessons of me or them.

THAT WAS MY DEAL BREAKER.

After so many breakups and heartaches after my Twin Flame died, I started to take time and evaluate myself on a deeper level and ask myself some of the hardest questions:

Why did I go out with him? Why did I like him? Why did I settle for that kind of treatment? Do I believe I deserve better? Did I do enough to deserve better? Do I deserve to be loved? Did I deserve what he did to me? Am I pretty enough for someone like him? Did I not require enough in myself? What was I not asking that I knew deep down I wanted? Am I not good enough to be someone's wife?

The other main reason most people begin to date and have a sexual relationship is due to undeniable physical attraction and levels of egoic conditions. A lot of the time people that are not emotionally able to accept their level of vulnerability and show that to others, will basically take whatever is offered to them. Most folks are deathly afraid of showing how they truly feel emotionally and will shut down all forces of themselves to their partner just for the sake of saving the partner's selfish pride and ego. Or they will remain emotionally shut down due to fear of being rejected. This is exactly how I used to measure my worth. I used to take whatever I was offered and whatever men said I was worthy enough for. I had such low self-esteem that I didn't even feel that my emotions were valid to express to my partners because each time I would, they would yell at me making me feel like I was in the wrong even though they made me feel that way.

Some people will say that you teach people how to treat you. This is especially true! During my time in dating as a Psychic Medium and after dealing with such darkened moments, I started to uncover that I wasn't commanding enough in myself because I just didn't feel like I deserved any better. I felt like no matter how much I tried or did, I'd never measure up to what other women got out of their men or their relationships and that I should just accept where I belonged. It was in facing Demons and negative men that I started realizing that there seemed to be a pattern from not just with what I was receiving from others, but what I was also accepting in myself.

SHOTGUN BREAKUP

One of the hardest, and most frightening relationships I've ever had was with a man I'll call "Mr. T". At first, he was sweet, charming and very attractive but there were times when he and I were together that just didn't add up.

He and I met sometime in 2014 in Fairbanks, Alaska which is nearly eight hours by car away from where I lived at the time. We met on a dating site and immediately felt an attraction for one another, but the more we exchanged conversations the more I started to sense something just wasn't right with him. At the time I wasn't aware of the warning signs, I was still naïve of the dating world and really wasn't sure what to make of the whole situation. And the fact he lived so far away from me should've already been a red flag, but I felt at the time that simply talking on the phone wouldn't be a big deal. Soon enough, we began to develop feelings for each other and would be on the phone for hours at a time.

When I first met "Mr. T", everything seemed sweet and simple. We both laughed and had fun with exchanging stories of our lives as young parents. On our first date while I happened to be staying in Fairbanks with my Aunt and Uncle, he let me drive his car in a parking lot. I was still learning to drive with the help of my Aunt at the age of twenty-seven. *(better late than never!)*.

When she heard that I was talking to "Mr. T" who happened to be working for a university, she was excited and offered generously for me to go on dates with him. I've not had a successful relationship in so long, so it felt like a good idea at the time. Our date was going so well that I didn't want it to end. He even surprised me with a yellow origami crane that he said he made for me. No one had ever done something like that for me before, and it felt genuine.

However, the suspicious part was he also revealed was newly separated and was in the middle of a divorce of his wife. Even then, I wasn't thinking of the possible reasons as to why he would be dating someone so soon. But I'll tell you -if I knew then, what I know now, I would've told myself to **run!**

Truth be told, he and I moved really fast. We dated for only a few months and decided to move in together but in order for us to do that, he had to move closer to me. When we made the decision to move in together, that's when I agreed to help him move out of his cabin.

You know that moment when you experience something for the first time and your mind is screaming, *"Get the fuck out of here?!"* -that was the moment when I first saw "Mr. T's" home. This was probably one of the biggest signs I could've gotten from the universe that I just chose to ignore simply because I really felt bad for the guy and wanted to try to make it work.

He was living in what he claimed to be a cabin with his son that was cute and cozy. But the truth was when I arrived at his cabin, I entered into a place full of garbage. I'm not talking about a few pieces of trash on the floor, some dirty dishes in the sink and maybe some clothes sprawled around the house, -this was a fucking landfill of **TRASH**. The amount of filth was so overwhelming, that I nearly threw up just being in his cabin because it was *that bad*. At the time, "Mr. T" also had a son that was still being potty trained so there were soiled diapers on the floor scattered pretty much everywhere!? It was so disgusting I looked at him and picked up a nail that was on the floor while looking at him saying...

ME:
"You know this is something people lose their kids over, right? This isn't safe for your son. I hope you realize this.
 -If you and I are going to be living together -there's no way this is going to be how we live."

As we began to clean out his cabin, I noticed a board game on the floor and I knew instantly what it was, and immediately walked out of the cabin. "Mr. T" knew what triggered me and said as he picked up the Ouija board…

MR. T:
"I'm sorry, I'll throw it in the dumpster right now."

Some say it's a stupid superstition, but I've had several negative experiences from spirits because of those boards. In fact, the moment I had stepped onto the property and got to the entrance of the cabin I sensed a negative energy that didn't sit right with me. The whole time I was there cleaning out his cabin I kept looking over to one of the corners of the place, sensing as if someone or *something*, was staring at me the whole duration I was there. Trying to be a good spouse for our new relationship I wanted to be supportive, so I did my best to remain in the cabin to clean but the whole time I knew something dark was there and it worried me.

The cabin was so warped from the mildew and mold from food, dirty diapers and God knows what else, (*that's a phrase I still use*) that we literally had to use shovels to clean out this guy's place. Not to mention there was a large tub in the middle of the living room that he used to bathe him and his son in because the cabin was like that of a studio apartment. There was only the one main room. His bedroom, kitchen, living room and bathroom were all in the same small square space he lived in within the walls of this cabin. I just couldn't believe it. I was so shocked by this I felt that it would be wrong of me not to try to somehow rescue him from this type of living situation, especially his young son.

What I think depressed me more was when I noticed he had an outhouse that he would use as a toilet. You know the kind you see in movies where there's a carved moon in the door, -well he literally carved a crescent moon into the door for his outhouse. The outhouse was a few feet away from his cabin and he would have to use a flashlight just to walk to the bathroom at night. That's probably one of the most redneck moments I've ever seen in my life. Being an Alaskan for more than twenty-two years, I can tell you that there's many types of folks you'll meet in AK, but one of the things that still gets me confused is why anyone would want to still live like they went back in time.

Give me a house with running water, a functioning toilet, kitchen, electricity and internet any day over this!

Thankfully his son didn't live with his father long and would only have weekend visits, that is until his ex-wife decided to move out of state with their son. Which is actually partially how he and I split up after only a few months living together because of what I said to him regarding his son. It's none of my business of what other parents do, even if I'm living with the same man and he's got kids from a previous relationship.

But what did get me concerned was when "Mr. T" would start confessing his anger towards his ex for leaving with their son, saying that it was selfish and that he will never be able to see his son again. I listened to everything he had to get off his chest, I must've listened to him for nearly an hour about this every day for weeks. But finally, I had to tell him what I saw from her perspective that I figured maybe he just wasn't seeing…

ME:

"Did it ever occur to you that maybe she's leaving state because all of her family is where she's going? You said she had no family in Alaska, how do you think that makes her feel when she's now a single mother raising a son by herself?"

He listened but I could tell he was only thinking about himself in this matter and it frankly pissed me off.

Me being a single mother of a daughter, I know it's not an easy decision to move to a whole other state to raise your children by yourself. I can't judge what his ex-wife had decided for herself, and frankly after how he treated me and why I had to breakup with him - *I don't blame her*. I think she made the right choice for what was better for her son. *And that's saying something.*

The reason why I say this is because during my relationship with "Mr. T", like I said, there were loads of red flags that I just couldn't seem to ignore. It got so often to the point that it would cause arguments between us a lot more than I had anticipated. Not only did I suspect he was cheating on me with another girl during the whole time we were dating, but that I was also experiencing severe nightmares nearly every night in our new apartment.

These nightmares would get to the extent where I'd wake up sweating and find scratches and bruises on my legs nearly every day. Even though I have anemia and need to take iron supplements, I knew this wasn't from anything like that, but I didn't want to admit that it could've been paranormal.

Throughout this relationship, I started to realize that the dark entity I sensed in his cabin had followed us to our new place. It was a male energy and it felt like it favored women, especially myself considering I had my third eye opened. Every few times I'd experience a bad dream and find another bruise, I'd mention it to "Mr. T", but it didn't seem to faze him. In fact, he almost seemed to just blow it off and didn't want to think about the possibility. It bothered me because then it made me feel like I was dealing with this entity alone even though we shared the same bed.

What was the most concerning was our fights. He and I rarely fought, and we always seemed to get along but the moment we moved in together we started having several fights a week to the point where we would be screaming and yelling at each other. Sometimes he would get so angry that he would throw things and break things and it frankly scared me.

This man was once a third-degree black belt in Taekwondo. He knew how to fight, and he could go from being a slow joe to lightening fast, without warning.

There were times in our arguments where his eyes would go pitch black during fights, that you couldn't even see the brown in his eyes anymore. He wasn't taking drugs, nor was he ever under the influence of anything that would make him react this way. He was diagnosed with bipolar disorder and he admitted refusing to take medication for it, because he didn't want to be like a "crazy person" having to take medicine for his disorder, (*those were his words, not mine*).

I've met plenty of folks with bipolar disorder but never has it ever gotten to the point where I had to worry for the safety of my life before. Intuitively I knew, something wasn't right.

Then one night we had our last and worst fight that literally caused us to break up. It was a moment so dark that it still makes me shaken up just mentioning it. It was also this moment that would change my perspective on the influence of demons and negative spirits forever.

It was on an afternoon where we were making dinner and going back to listening to "Mr. T" complain about his ex-wife leaving with their son. Listening to this for a repeated amount of times it came to the point where I finally told him what I knew he didn't want to hear…

ME:
"I'm just guna say it even though I know it's going to piss you off. But you need to stop being a baby about this and man the fuck up…"

He was shocked at what I said and turned to me confused…

ME:
"-You're a grown ass man with just yourself to worry about now. If you really love your son and want to be in your son's life, then move to where she's moving. Otherwise, stop bitching about it. If you don't want to make the adult choice in sacrificing where you live to be with your son, then you don't really love him the way you should as a parent because it's about sacrifice and…"

-Before I could even finish my sentence, he then grabbed a knife along with a pair of chopsticks in his hand and put them up to my throat. The ability he had to get from being super calm to suddenly threatening me with a knife to my throat was astounding. There wasn't even time for me to react to get away because he was *that fast*. I've never met someone, nor have I ever dated someone to threaten me in this way. Knowing my daughter was also in the same room with us I knew I had to also make wise choices for every second counted. That's when calmly I said but as stern as I possibly could...

ME:
"...Back up...and get away from me...***now***."

My daughter only being a toddler at the time, looked at me quite frightened. That's when I told her to go to her room and shut the door. When she did, all he could do was say that I wasn't being fair to him...

MR. T:
"Don't you ever talk about my son like that again! Don't you *ever* say I don't love my son!"

That's all he could say over and over. In his eyes as he spoke were total black holes. He was a totally different person that I didn't recognize.

I knew that my daughter's safety was my ultimate responsibility and that I made a promise that I'd die for her to keep her safe even if that meant getting my throat cut open. -*Of course*, I wanted to make sure that didn't happen.

What most people won't expect about me is I may be small, and I may not win in a physical fight at all. But when it comes to my children or any child's wellbeing, I will do *whatever* it takes to make sure they're safe, even if that means I get hurt in the process. The point of being a mother or a father, is you make a vow in your heart of hearts that you not only bring them in this world to love, guide and teach them things in life, but to protect them through our animalistic nature. There's a lion that comes into play when you realize someone is messing with your cub, and that's when you have to decide when it's necessary to take the claws out.

This moment was all about tact, however. I knew that if I was going to get out of this, I'd have to remain calm and clear in my decisions. That's when I proceeded to back away from the knife that was still pointing to my throat and continued by saying…

ME:

"If you don't get away from me, I *will* call the police. I have my daughter here and what you're doing is now considered abuse."

He kept walking toward me each time I took a step backward and that's when I got angry and knew I had to confront the situation...

ME:

"Are you going to stab me?! Is that what you're going to do?! This is now considered abuse, and this isn't something I tolerate. *BACK THE FUCK UP OR I'LL CALL THE POLICE!*"

It was here he backed up and then in one swift motion took a pot of boiling hot water and threw it into the sink. I then ran to my daughter's bedroom and shut the door behind me. Her and I stayed in the bedroom the rest of the night. It scared her from what he did and had to calm her down until she fell asleep.

The other concern I was faced with was there was no lock on the bedroom door so I tried to position one of her dressers up against the door to make sure he couldn't get in. But the dresser was too heavy to lift or move by myself so I'd sit in front of the door praying he wouldn't come in.

Here is where it may sound strange to those not used to how energy works, but I was so desperate for safety for my daughter and

I, that I took a finger and made a line on the rug in front of the door. As I did, I said the words with all of my energy saying,

"Only love, light and positive energy and positive people with positive intentions may cross this line."

I must've said this a dozen times while making a line with my finger of intended sealing energy. I never heard of this type of sealing before, nor did I really know what I was doing, but somewhere deep inside I intuitively felt the desperate need to do this with the help of energy from the universe to keep us safe.

There were times he tried to come into the room, but I told him I didn't want to talk to him. Each time he tried to apologize I told him we were done, and that I'd be leaving the next day. He knew that abuse isn't tolerable for me and that no matter what his excuse was, I wasn't going to allow that kind of abuse to be around my daughter.

By the time Josslyn fell asleep, the sun had already been set and all within the apartment seemed quiet. I then walked to the door to see if maybe "Mr. T" had gone to sleep, so that I could get our bags made to be ready by early morning to leave. But the moment I exited her bedroom, I noticed all of the lights in the apartment were off. Not a light was on, except for a slight beam reaching into the living room near the entrance from an outside streetlight. As I examined the space in the hall, I noticed a dark figure in the living room sitting quietly in a chair positioned up against the front door of the apartment. It was "Mr. T", sitting in a chair holding a beer in one hand and his loaded shotgun in the other.

Some people have asked what was going on in my mind when I saw the shotgun in his hand. To be honest, I was **HORRIFIED**. The only thing that kept repeating in my head was the image of a headline from a news article that said,

"BOYFRIEND SHOOTS GIRLFRIEND AND DAUGHTER, THEN PUTS GUN ON HIMSELF."

All I could think about in that moment was my daughter and I were goners if I didn't play this out ***right*** as best as humanly possible. I still shake thinking about this. This was not a normal situation for me, because I was raised without guns in the house, so handling a gun wasn't on my to-do list. I didn't know how to even handle a gun, let alone prevent a person from using one. But I've heard enough stories, seen enough documentaries from police scenarios about this type of situation so I *felt* I knew how to handle it. I knew that I had to remain calm.

Instantly I examined his position of where he had placed himself intentionally. He sat directly in front of the main door of the apartment to stop me from leaving, so I knew that this was his way of control. I've heard from women and men from their stories about abusive relationships, that say the biggest threat about abusive spouses is when their significant other tries to leave the relationship. That factor played in my mind, realizing in that exact second that I was in an abusive relationship and I had to **GET OUT**!

But the way I did it, will probably make you think that I'm completely nuts. Not knowing what the hell I was going to do, I asked Yehoshua for help immediately. I begged as loud as I could in my mind, pleading and hoping I'd get the right help from Angels, or from some type of higher help to get us out of this safely. And when I did, the oddest answer echoed inside my thoughts and all I could hear was, *"call him on his bluff. Scare him with the truth..."* And I did just that...

ME:
"What are you trying to do? What is this...?"

I asked as calm as I possibly could in hopes he wouldn't hear my fear escaping my voice. Not looking up from his gun he answered in a monotone...

MR. T:
"I just think that if I can't have you or my son, what is the point in living anymore..."

I knew the risk, but my gut told me to do what I was told...

ME:

"Well, that's a pretty selfish thing to do. -That's a great idea. Kill yourself so your son never knows who his father is and then he will forever wonder if you even loved him at all and why you didn't care enough to see him get married, go to college or anything important in his life. But if you're guna kill yourself, hurry it up because I got shit to pack."

I walked back into the room knowing full well that he could've shot me, Josslyn and then put the gun on himself. However, I also knew that by mentioning the negative impact it would have on his son, would stir an awareness inside of him that would eat away at the thought of suicide in general.

I speak about suicide from a personal level for I've struggled with suicidal thoughts in the past. I've dealt with depression after having been raped several times that made me just want to end all of the pain. That's what happens with depression, when you focus so much on your pain, loss and the levels of unfairness in yourself and from the struggle that you completely forget those that love you.

No way am I suggesting that suicide should ever be encouraged. I *never* say this to a person, in fact, I've talked several people closest to me, including clients out of suicide. I've spoken to a person who had a gun to their head to put the gun down while on the phone with this person to not do it, -but I'll tell you it was one of the scariest calls

I've ever had in my life. Suicide is one of the worst killers and should always be taken seriously **every time**.

In "Mr. T's" case, I knew he was doing it for attention, control and for fear. I knew intuitively he wasn't going to do it. The truth is, I've learned from many experiences that if a person was absolutely serious about ending their own life, they won't tell a soul about it -they'll just do it. But if a person is contemplating the thought of committing suicide, will usually speak to someone about it when they're fearful of doing so. But this wasn't the case. He was using this as a threat to keep me in the relationship which is another form of neglect and emotional abuse. I've learned this from watching and learning much from psychologists and those that have survived abusive relationships and their spouses.

And even though he may have seemed genuine on committing the act against himself, there was a stillness inside of me that psychicly *knew* he was more fearful of death than he led on. I just knew deep down he didn't want to end his life, he just wanted to control me in any desperate measure that he could.

Like I've said, suicide is a very serious thing and should **never** be encouraged. I didn't encourage him as it may have appeared that way. I didn't tell him to do it, I said, "if you do", which implied I wasn't going to stop him from his own free will choice. Of course, I said what was necessary to prevent him from doing it and to think twice about how it will impact his family and his son for the rest of his life.

But ultimately, I basically scared him with a taste of reality, and because of that, he went to bed and went to work the next day.

I knew that leaving "Mr. T" was the right thing to do, not just because of what he attempted and how he behaved that night, but also from many other red flags that also led me to know he wasn't being faithful.

Eventually I also found out during our relationship that he was cheating on me with another girl in Fairbanks, Alaska whenever he was going on "business trips" -which I knew was bullshit. I knew he was cheating on me because I'd also catch him talking, or texting someone and the moment I'd notice or wake up from sleep he would immediately shut off his phone or hide it from me. Not to mention when he was having his divorce court, he said we could stay in his *"friends"* house who was gone for work for a few weeks. "Mr. T" confessed later in the relationship that his wife divorced him because he was cheating on her, and of course it was with the same girl I suspected he was cheating on me with.

I'm not the type of jealous person to immediately suspect infidelity just because you have a girl that's a friend, that's not my character. I have loads of guy friends that I care deeply about and feel that having relationships with men and women is important for soul growth as long as it's genuine, honest and respectful.

What got me to the suspicion is when we arrived at his *"friend's"* house, I quickly learned it was a woman's home from how neat and clean it appeared. When we walked into the house, I heard the words in the motion of pictures saying, *"Go to the kitchen"* in telepathy. The moment I approached the kitchen I felt the need to turn around to face the kitchen wall to my left, and there on the wall tacked on a tack board where one can tack notes, was a yellow origami crane. The same crane he had made me, was also the same one he gave her. It crushed me. I knew the truth even in that moment. I knew he had still been seeing her, and that he was using the same tricks on me just like he did her.

Though I knew this was enough of evidence to support my suspicions I still stayed with him but not without saying, as I pointed to the crane, "So, your tricks work on all the girls huh?" He just looked at me like the idiot he was.

VICTORIA

After our breakup, I later found out I was pregnant, but had later lost our daughter when I was about three months along. I had lost her in the toilet after I had felt something different within my womb, and when I went to attempt to use the restroom, the slightest push caused her to fall from inside my womb into the toilet bowl. It took everything in me to sum up the ability to shout to my mother who was visiting, to come and get my daughter's remains out of the toilet and call for an ambulance.

Losing her was extremely hard on me. I struggled with the loss for many years and still miss her every day wondering what it would've been like if I had her. There are times where I'm convinced it was my fault that she didn't make it, for there was an instance where I had stretched too far and caused a rip from inside my stomach. The rip caused massive bleeding and was told by my OBGYN that there was a 50/50 chance of losing her. I knew from the loss of blood there was no way she was going to make it. A mother knows this kind of thing just from common sense. It angers me greatly that doctors still try to lie, especially when there's really no way she was going to live. I knew it, and they knew it.

After losing my daughter, Victoria, (*I named her because no matter what, she will forever be my daughter*), I knew that I'd have to deal with many other dynamics to the loss like depression, PTSD and anxiety especially after the trauma from "Mr. T".

It's never easy when you lose a child. But as difficult as it was mentally and emotionally, my abilities gifted me the healing in seeing her spirit in dreams several times a year. Mending our relationship and bond as mother and daughter, gave me the opportunity to heal faster than I ever could've anticipated and am forever grateful.

DATING A DEMONOLOGIST

Probably one of the more challenging things in my life is people understanding my lifestyle as a Demonologist. I get loads of misunderstood judgement calls from folks with things like, "Why are you so dark?" or, "You know you attract demons because you talk about them right?" or my favorite, "You're a witch and a whore of the devil."

Being a Demonologist doesn't mean that I like talking about demons or that I'm attracted to them. I learned I was meant to be a Demonologist because of the amount of attacks I've had, and I simply got tired of it. I decided that learning about negative spirits would help me and then I learned it would help others.

After my breakup with "Mr. T", I started to uncover that the reason he more than likely behaved in such outrageous ways was due to the negative entity that was influencing him in our apartment. I also learned that entity became attached to "Mr. T" when he used his Ouija board. It targeted him and used him as a pawn in order to gain control of our relationship in order to ponder up more fear from me through the manipulation of "Mr. T's" rage. That's what dark spirits do. They feed off of our fear by using our emotions and then amplifying our anger ten times more than how we normally would react.

I know this not just from that relationship experience but from many other ex's I've dated that I'd later find out also had negative spirit's attached to them. More often I'd discover that after I would meet certain men, I'd find out that they had a negatively charged spirit lingering in their home or was fully attached to them and somehow always found their way to me.

People say that I attract negative people because that's a reflection of myself, but this isn't the case as a Demonologist. When a person decides to become a Demonologist, they're making a declaration on an energetic level that they're going to become something similar like a cop on the astral realms. Something like a police officer that works on the astral realm and patrols both the physical realm and the ethereal realm for the protection of the living and the dead. That's it in a nutshell how I describe and view it contemporarily.

However, there's much of the opinion from those of a more religious nature that view it as heresy. But it's just simply not. It's just another way to help people in order to keep the balance between both realms to help alleviate the possible chaos that can and *does* occur if not handled immediately. And it's because of this ignorance that causes a lot of people to judge so quickly and assume that I bring nothing but bad news everywhere I go. But if they spent even as much as a day in my shoes, they'd never say that to my face or behind my back again.

As a Demonologist, dating is especially complicated due to the reality that my life is targeted on a daily basis from negative energies like demons, earth bound souls, familiar spirits and even devils of a diabolical nobility. The moment someone remotely hears that I mention this, they laugh thinking it's ridiculous, but it's something that even the famous Paranormal Investigators, **ED AND LORRAINE WARREN** vouched for in many texts and editorials where they've mentioned the same level of an *astral hit* on their heads.

Demons and other negative forces don't like to be told they can't haunt specific people, and they most definitely **DON'T** like it when you step up to their level of awareness with the full intention of stopping them. Demons absolutely **HATE** this without apologies and will stop at nothing to make sure your voice and abilities are silenced at every level possible. People that are **SLEEPERS** (*people that haven't awakened*) simply just don't understand this metaphysical threat unless they've been faced with this type of entity at least once in their life.

The threat is **REAL**, and it's because of this threat that it's my undivided soul responsibility to make that reality known to any and all people that choose to associate with me. If I didn't let people know this in advance I wouldn't be caring about their wellbeing. It would be irresponsible if I didn't make this known to all people that either want to be my friend, or that is interested in courting me. *(Does anyone even court anymore?)*

Unfortunately, because of this, I've been told by many Psychic Mediums that I'd be alone for the majority of my life, and more than likely will never be married - **FIGURES**.

MELINDA KAY LYONS

Being a Demonologist and trying to date isn't easy because it's not exactly the subtle conversation you want to tell someone what it is you exactly do. When people picture the word **DEMONOLOGIST**, they most often think of something like the exorcism films or paranormal movies that make you never want to enter a haunted house or use a Ouija board again. Granted Hollywood is famous for exaggerating truth from reality when it comes to the paranormal and nearly everything else, but I'd be lying if I said it was all fake. I can't tell you how many times men broke up with me, because of paranormal things they'd start having when I would spend the night. The core aspect to why this occurs though is not what most people judge. These spiritual attacks don't happen because I attracted it, they happen because the entities want me to continue to be alone, to feel alone through continual rejection. This is a game they play to put the person's emotions into a negative aspect so as to conjure toxic feelings that could sabotage my work, focus, self-belief, purpose and anything remotely positive.

And though a lot of the times demons have been successful for scaring some of these men away, it's not stopped nor deterred me from continuing to expose the truth. It's because of these demons that it's become my divine purpose and life mission to unveil what they're about and why we should never fear them -but face them with all of the power we possess within us.

DEMON DEALER

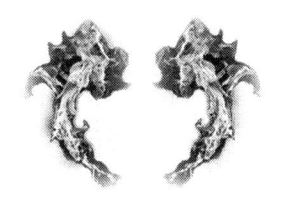

A FEW WEEKS AFTER "MR. T" AND I BROKE UP, HE CONTACTED ME THROUGH FACEBOOK TRYING TO APOLOGIZE AGAIN. AND IT WAS IN THIS CONVERSATION THAT HE RELAYED THAT SINCE THAT NIGHT HE COULD NEVER BRING HIMSELF TO STEP FOOT INTO THAT ROOM AFTER WE LEFT, OR SINCE.

I **NEVER** TOLD HIM WHAT I DID 'TILL AFTER HIS CONFESSION

MELINDA KAY LYONS

PARANORMAL ADVISORY

WHO YOU GUNA CALL?

One of the most common questions I get asked from fans and even skeptics is, *"Why Demonology?"* There are several reasons why I'm focused more on demons and negative spirits -but it's not the purpose most people usually presume.

The definition of **DEMONOLOGY** in the *Wikipedia* states:

"Demonology is the study of demons or beliefs about demons, especially the methods used to summon and control them."

This is true to an extent. However, there's a much longer definition to be added here. Most of the population are under the notion that when one is in the study or relation to demonology, that this immediately suggests or identifies the person to be associating themselves with demons and devils on a personal level. Placing a label similar to like a satanic association where the demonologist's intention is to work **with** the demons, not against them. This is **FALSE**.

My overall intention and focus in the pursuit of demonology is to understand the negative forces as much as soulfully and energetically as possible. The more knowledge and information I learn and receive from further experience from the dark energies, gives me further answers to how to help people on a grander energetic and psychic scale from the malevolence.

Let's be real, most Psychic Mediums and people that claim to be "sensitives" don't like to admit there's a dark force at work and will even tell clients that they're causing the issues, even to the level that they've attracted the evil to themselves. This pisses me off on so many levels that honestly, it makes me want to sit all of their asses down and show them how wrong they are. This is not only completely wrong, but makes people feel ashamed and responsible of a demon attacking them in the first place. How a person can sit in front of another and tell them they're causing it is beyond me.

The only time this would be the case, is if the person was summoning and contacting Demons intentionally, like through the use of a Ouija board, séances or through dark rituals.

In my line of work, I offer a special type of service called **PARANORMAL ADVISORY**, where I use my abilities completely free of charge. Helping people from all over the world. I've had clients from New York, Washington, Oregon, California, Florida, Alaska and all the way to Australia, Ireland, Iran, Sweden and many other locations. Though the line of requests from fans and others that trust in my ability to help them has been humbling, it's my passion and ultimate focus to ensure that they're left with answers to their questions and concerns. However, in the beginning when I first started working professionally, I never thought in a million years that my work would be to deal with demon issues.

When I started working in my career as a Psychic Medium, I thought I was meant to be those Psychic Mediums you'd see on TV or read about: *Theresa Caputo, the Long Island Medium, James Van Praagh,* or like *Tyler Henry, The Hollywood Medium.*

I used to offer my abilities to help people connect with their departed loved ones in hopes to help alleviate their pain and grief from the loss, but over time I started to notice an uncomfortable commonality with more than half of my client requests. Originally the requests were to connect with a departed loved one or for spiritual counsel but then I'd uncover they were haunted by a negatively charged spirit and it was causing them harm emotionally, mentally, and even physically. It would happen so often to the point I'd have to turn the session more into paranormal focus first and then after it was addressed, I would give the client the session experience they contacted me for originally. The more clients I scheduled the more I paid close attention to this bizarre coincidence each and every time. What would be even more alarming would be when a client's departed loved one would begin telling me about the demon or negative spirit that was hurting their loved one (my client) and would ask me to help them. It would be so often that it didn't take long for me to add *Paranormal Advisory* to my list of services.

LEA

In March 2015, a woman named Lea contacted me after finding me through Facebook and had noticed I was a newly Psychic Medium offering free readings. When she contacted me, she mentioned that she was also living in Alaska, and so we made an appointment to meet somewhere quiet and agreed to meet at a local library. Looking back on it now, I don't know why I'd do a reading for a client in a library, but I needed to be in a place that no one would interrupt the session.

When we arrived at the library, we went to the second floor and seated ourselves at a table a little away from folks walking around or studying so we wouldn't get disturbed and wouldn't bother others. Lea agreed in allowing me the chance to video record her session being that it was an even exchange of her getting a free session and me having the reading documented. It was exciting for me. I never had anyone let me do this before, so I was nervous on whether or not I'd not only be good at what I do, but make a legitimate connection with her departed loved one.

When we sat down and started the session, I began to pick up a few things and confessed that a few pieces of images and thoughts were arriving in my mind since that very morning. Telling her that when I was even brushing my teeth to get myself ready, spirit was already giving me thoughts and emotions guided by images to let me know what Lea was possibly going through. It was confusing to me and didn't quite make sense at first, but I knew it had something to do with her work. When I said this, she busted into a laugh followed by shock. That's when she admitted that she wanted to test my abilities when she agreed to having her reading.

Lea began getting goosebumps followed with emotions flushing her face red as she said someone would call her name at work on a daily basis when no one was around…

LEA:

"I was walking down the back hall, and I heard probably about five feet behind me, a very loud whisper. *"Lea"*, very clearly."

When she began expressing this paranormal happening, that's when a male energy started to reach into my awareness of psychic sensory and I knew it was someone like a family member. When I made this sense known to her, she paused as I asked…

ME:

"I'm sensing a male energy that is around you and is connected to you and is with us now."

Instantly that's when Lea confirmed that she had lost her brother who died at the age of thirty-five, from skin cancer. In her reading experience we both got something positive from this.

Lea was able to know that her brother's soul was still alive and watching over her, and I was able to have my very first reading experience documented to build my credibility. This was huge to me. This was like receiving an award in a way because this was more than just a video to me, this was trust being built from one person that would grow into many. I knew this intuitively. I heard on a regular basis that this experience wasn't going to be my last, and more so, wasn't going to be the only case where a spirit outside the family was interacting with the client. Her gift in trust enabled me further confidence to keep going and to trust in myself.

Granted, we originally agreed to her session being free of charge. But of course, Lea being so kind, still sneaked money into my damn hand and laughed as she left and wouldn't let me give it back. Forever I'll always remember this reading with Lea. It was an emotional experience that I'll never forget and will remain grateful for her trust, and permission to channel her brother's soul.

This was a prominent moment for me because it gave me the chance to begin identifying the energetic differences from specific souls on different levels of vibrations, intentions and purposes during a session. Though I was still new at learning the energetic differences, I started to recognize how my body would begin reacting negatively or positively to the souls I'd be connecting with. Each vibration whether positive, negative or neutral have intricately different energetic vibrational pulses that will trigger the body in multiple ways. Over the course of further practice with other people and reading into their experiences, it was this unveiling of truth that I'd learn how to cope and relay these responses to clients, friends and even strangers I'd happen to meet by chance.

WICKED MAGIC

There's an experience with a person whom I used to know for a long time. We will call her, "Ms. A". She and I go way back to our childhood. Both of our moms knew one another for a long time and so that's how we began our friendship but due to this one moment, I knew we couldn't associate any longer. Granted, I don't hate her, nor do I judge her on her chosen path, however as a Psychic Medium, I knew that what she was doing was not only putting herself in jeopardy but was also negatively impacting my family.

It happened back in 2015 where she and I started reconnecting after a time of drifting apart. We never intended to stop talking at first, life just happened where she was making her life and I was busy raising my daughter Josslyn as a single mother. But there was a day where I went to her apartment to visit her and rekindled the memories from childhood and laugh like we used to.

The whole night went great, we didn't have any issues. However, the whole time I was there I couldn't help but sense a negative energy while at the same time, seeing a dark figure watching our every move. The energy would be so uncomfortable to the point where I hated being in her place. I almost felt suffocated. The entity that I'd keep seeing in my third eye made me extremely uneasy to the point I hated going to the bathroom or even undressing. There were instances where I swear, I felt like someone had smacked my ass, poked my sides and even pulled my hair. It felt as if I was being violated the entire time, I was in her apartment. After a few hours in her apartment, I finally asked...

ME:

"Did you do witchcraft in your home? I keep feeling like something negative is in your house and I'm not sure why I keep feeling this."

"Ms. A" looked at me a bit shocked but then denied by saying she's not done anything negative to attract evil in her home intentionally. She did confess that she had some tarot cards but nothing negative or dark was being done in her home. Trying to trust her I let the concern go as best as I could. But when it came time to sleeping, I kept getting woken up by a dark entity that would lay on top of me. Eventually it took my astral body, dragged me around on the roof and proceed to hurt me on the astral realm. At the time I didn't understand that this was an astral attack, but looking back on it now, that's definitely what it was.

After that I made the decision to never sleep in her apartment again. And good thing too because over the course of a few months later she ended up calling me desperate for help.

She knew that I was new to my abilities and coming into my own style as a Psychic Medium. She hoped that perhaps I could give her a reading on the paranormal things happening that frankly were freaking her out. She was so fearful on the phone that I couldn't help but shake the whole time. Not only was I sensing her anxiety, but later I'd learn I was also sensing the negative spirit's presence. It was then I told her to give me at least two weeks to have the spirit come to me so I could see what she was going through. Little did I know that this would be my first official *Paranormal Advisory* session with a Demon.

When I asked her what was going on, that's when she told me that she's been seeing a dark shadowy figure in her home at night with glowing red eyes. Along with things happening that made her scream from the occurrences feeling as if they were intended to frighten her:

- DOORS OPENING, CLOSING BY THEMSELVES
- LOUD FOOTSTEPS WALKING DOWN THE HALLWAY
- DOORKNOBS TURNING, RATTLING BY THEMSELVES
- HEARING KNOCKS, BANGS IN 3'S
- SMELLING ROTTEN MEAT, ROTTEN EGGS
- CONSTANT NIGHTMARES OF MURDER, RAPE, INCLUDING BEING ATTACKED BY MONSTERS

- WAKING UP WITH BRUISING AND SCRATCH MARKS
- FEELING AS IF SOMEONE IS RAPING HER IN THE MIDDLE OF THE NIGHT WHEN SLEEPING

Not only did "Ms. A" list all of these things, I started to experience a similar commotion. The paranormal activity would become so unbearable, that I would have to sleep in my daughter's room at night. Josslyn, being young at the time, was waking up screaming from horrible nightmares nearly each night that she refused to sleep without me. She'd say someone in her dreams was trying to continually hurt her. Describing while crying with immense amounts of fear and anxiety of the scary faces of "monsters" with claws chasing and harming her in her dreams.

Being a mother, it not only greatly concerned me for my daughter's wellbeing but also for her safety. There were also mornings when she would be getting dressed that we would find scratches and bruises on her body. As a mom this was *extremely* difficult to see because I wanted her to be safe, but *what could I do?* I was just another human being barely knowing how I would even remotely handle a situation like this -let alone solve it.

Without a doubt it became clear as the days went by that "Ms. A" was dealing with a Demon in her home. Doors would be opening and closing in my house without any explanation, but I would also start seeing dark shadowy figures at the corner of my eye. There were moments in the night where I'd hear knocks that'd wake me up from a deep and disturbing nightmare yet again, and again. The terror grew more disturbing as the fear grew which I wasn't entirely aware of yet for I was only a newbie in the demonology field. It wasn't something I was necessarily trained to do, but I knew after reading some of the demonology books I had in my study that there were too many correlations in each paranormal disturbance.

What got me next, knocked me to the floor -**LITERALLY**. There was a morning I'll never forget, and it was something I really didn't think was remotely possible medically, scientifically, spiritually or even logically. I had woken up one morning after having another terrible nightmare and when I tried to stand up, I noticed my energy within myself felt completely sucked dry. I could barely keep my eyes open and the moment I attempted to stand on my feet, my legs had given up on me without a warning and I collapsed on the floor **HARD**. It hurt a lot. I remember shouting from the pain when realizing that my face had nearly met with the floor, but thankfully my hands were able to catch my face in the fall. Opening my heavy lids, I stumbled to try to stand but I just couldn't. All of my might I tried to stand but felt completely paralyzed from the waist down.

Though I could feel my toes and legs, for some bizarre reason, I had no strength in my legs or hips to position myself upright. My daughter had to get my computer chair and push it towards me so I could climb onto the chair and move around as if it were a wheelchair.

The bigger trouble I faced were the stairs in the house. My bedroom was downstairs and walking up and down the stairs became exceedingly difficult and no less painful. I'd be screaming from the pain accompanied in my hips as if I were run over by a car. There were several times I'd have no choice but to crawl on my hands and knees just to get around the house because I was not only in extreme pain but too weak to stand. Even though I felt paralyzed, there was a lot of pain ringing in my waist and legs with every move I made and couldn't figure out what had caused it.

To put it straight, I felt like something seriously wrong was happening to my health as it took several days to stand and walk normally again. I even took myself to a local clinic to get checked out but after doing several tests the doctor couldn't find anything to explain how and why this happened.

Even though I'm a firm believer and *knower* of the afterlife and of spiritualistic attacks, one should seek immediate medical attention in order to dissect any and all possible root causes for things that can be debunked or explained. The moment it can't be explained by doctors or science, that's when one should resort to the possibility of it being a paranormal phenomenon.

Once my ability to walk normally was substantial, I knew that it was time to talk to "Ms. A" again and tell her what I had experienced and give her a formal reading. Though she had informed me of a few things prior, remember, she didn't pay for the session and I had specifically told her not to tell me anything else that would influence her reading.

When we did have the reading, I started to see the word, *"witchcraft"* again in my mind. It wouldn't leave. Each time I kept pushing the word and ritual ideas out of my head, it kept coming back, so I finally let it out and told her...

ME:

"I know I asked you before, but I keep seeing the word, *"witchcraft"* or something dark being done in your home. It won't leave my mind. - you better be up front and tell me what the hell is going on and what you did because I know that this wouldn't keep popping up from Spirit if it wasn't true."

At that point I was getting angry. Even though she had denied it the first time, I knew she wasn't being fully honest with me.

"Ms. A" breathed deeply and after a long sigh, she then finally came out and regrettably admitted to doing rituals involving witchcraft.

When I heard this, it started to make not only a lot of sense, it reassured me further that my ability to read the situation was more correct than I realized. The more I read into her situation, the more I presented to her, the harder it was for her to process this reality check. It seemed as if to her I was making it all up, that is until I let her know about my legs giving out and that's when she nearly burst into tears.

The undeniable connection between her experiences and mine were mind blowing. Apparently, she had been going to the doctor for months due to her legs suddenly not working properly and she would be unable to walk for weeks. When she went to several doctors, they all said they couldn't find the root of what caused her legs to be in this paralysis state. Being that we weren't as close, I was never aware of her health in the slightest.

The more I listened as she spoke about her health, the more worried I became. It was obvious the entity in her home was slowly killing her, for she was suffering more health complications that doctors said most people don't face 'till they're in their fifties -but she was in her mid-twenties. Her health was not only deteriorating exceptionally fast, but she had moments of temporary blindness where she wouldn't be able to see anything. It would take what felt like forever for her to see again. Granted the doctors did find considerable amounts of tests focused on her health that were explaining things like the blindness, but what stumbled the experts, was the health complications just suddenly appeared without any significant warning nor a clear explanation. As for the walking trouble, the doctors still couldn't find a reason for it and made "Ms. A" wonder if she was just losing her mind or even dying.

Eventually in the reading rapid flashes of images began to emerge into my mind where I was seeing what looked like a gargoyle. When I described this image to her of the demon, again she began screaming and crying because she then admitted she had been dreaming of this same gargoyle with glowing red eyes. In one dream specifically, she described how she went to sleep on her couch only to see the entity in her living room staring back at her.

Unsure of what to do, she asked it what it was, and why it was there. The entity spoke in return saying that it was her "guardian angel" and that it was there to answer the questions she had. However, when she described the gargoyle's appearance, she said it was nearly all black with red eyes and its voice frankly scared the shit out of her.

It took several minutes in convincing "Ms. A" that she was being tricked by a malevolent dark entity -a demon. Advising her that it would be wise to get rid of the books and all of the dark ritualistic artifacts she used in the spells or conjuring rituals. The reading must've been nearly two hours on the phone, but she reluctantly agreed to do what I suggested and to cleanse her home immediately. I also advised her to call onto Angels to help her health and to secure her safety from the demon in her home.

DEMON DEALER

A few weeks went by and I hadn't heard from her. Deep down I knew there was something still not right with herself energetically and unfortunately my instincts were spot on. The next time and last time I heard from her, she said she didn't do what I advised, and claimed that what she was doing wasn't inviting the demon. Her main excuse was the spells she was doing were only based on herbs and other healing measures.

Knowing "Ms. A" as long as I have, I knew she still had the entity in her home because that same demon would show up again even after talking with her on the phone that one time. It got me so enraged at how irresponsible and unsafe this was that I told her my peace and said I couldn't associate myself with someone that chooses to live with demons and play in the dark arts.

Crossing the line in deciding when to put up that safety barrier when associating with others can be exceptionally challenging, especially when you love the person. But keeping my distance from her I feel was the best decision I could make for the safety of my daughter, family and myself. Demons don't just show up at your house because you've done a few herb spells for healing, and they sure as hell don't arrive in your living room after doing a few love spells. The issue here is she was in complete denial of just how serious this ordeal was and possibly still is.

Hoping I'm wrong and she's gutted that thing out and cut it out of her life completely. But do I feel that I can trust a person who's chosen that life for themselves to make the same choices for me? No. I'll admit that I yelled on the phone because I just couldn't believe that after all of what she was going through that she would choose to still let the demon haunt and terrorize her the way it was. It was literally, physically **KILLING** her slowly to the point where she couldn't walk or see when she was only in her mid-twenties.

After much tests, she did reveal that she was diagnosed with an illness (I seriously can't remember what it is) but most folks that are diagnosed with this illness are considerably much older than her. The facts were there. The entity was causing her health to deteriorate right before her very eyes. But even with all of this evidence, she still wouldn't take my advice. Not only is this irresponsible but downright foolish and I just couldn't and won't let someone like that come into my life that chooses to work with demons.

A FATHER'S POSSESSION

Sometime in October 2017, I was contacted by a man named Dave who had contacted me for a free session in hopes to have a few things answered for him. He didn't tell me anything about what he was experiencing, except that he needed to understand a few things and wished to also connect with a departed loved one. Not aware of who he was referring to, nor did I know what he needed guidance or help on, I took the time to schedule him and waited for a few weeks to see what I'd experience in my Psychic Medium abilities.

Between the time of scheduling him and before the session occurred, not much was going on, except that I had a very disturbing dream. I was in a man's house and found that there were two demons controlling him. It was so lucid that I could smell rotten flesh, and see blood all over the walls, the floor and flesh was scattered throughout the area of the space. I remember waking up knowing all too well that Dave was either in serious danger, or that the person in the dream was possibly his departed family member.

When Dave and I started his session, he had given me permission to video record his reading experience and share it on my *YouTube* channel, *Last Frontier Medium*. When I do share video recording experiences of clients, it's strictly for educational purposes to help others that may be having similar experiences and need reassurance that they're not crazy and how to get help. I never monetize or make money on the videos and share them for individuals to learn from another person's experience.

Like always, I was eternally grateful for the gift in reading his life with trust in my ability, but I wanted to make sure that what I was reading was as accurate as possible. I'll admit his reading was challenging. It took longer than usual because the negative spirits were blocking my ability in seeing clearly to identify what was going on. Once I was able to gain enough energy and focus with the help of my **SPIRIT GUIDES**, I was then shown that Dave's father's soul was the departed soul he was hoping to have answers to. After establishing this connection with my guides, the information started to flood in faster and clearer.

During the reading I was able to identify the two demonic entities that were not only a part of his father's life turmoil, but negative influences from severe alcohol abuse. His father had been an alcoholic for a big portion of his life up to his death. Once this came to light it all started to make sense. Days prior to his session, I'd get severe dizzy spells. The dizziness was so overwhelming that I'd literally run into walls and fall to the floor a few times because I felt as if I were heavily intoxicated. I hadn't had any alcohol during this timeline because I like to make sure that everything that I'm experiencing is authentic and paranormally genuine as much as humanly possible.

Upon establishing this intoxicating connection (pun intended), that's when I shared with Dave another astral projection experience I had. During my astral projection experience, Dave's father had walked up a flight of stairs and was walking towards Dave. The moment I had seen his father, I knew there was something terribly wrong. His father's eyes were blackened and hooked with a fierce stare as if not looking from a human soul but from something else that took over him. His father began speaking in different languages, accents, along with the tone of his voice continually changing pitch as if uncontrollably. This was unlike anything I've witnessed and knew this was a possession situation. For his father's behavior wasn't of his character that seemed natural nor human, including in the sight of his posture as he carried himself. It almost seemed like something of an animal or as if he were under control of something **INHUMAN**.

Not only was the astral projection a nearly intolerable Psychic jolt of information but so were the many Mediumship experiences before the session. I would taste blood throughout the week before Dave's reading. The taste of blood would happen as I'd lay down to sleep and would begin coughing as if I were choking from my own blood. It scared me a few times being that I wasn't sure if it could become harmful to me as I slept. Adding to the Psychic stain, I'd receive what felt like jabs or blows to my head. Each blow to the head caused severe headaches that I'd have to take over the counter pain medicine to alleviate the waves of displeasure.

Informing Dave of what I've seen was difficult because no one wants to know that their family member was possibly under some level of demonic influence or possession. But it was my job, it's what I signed up to do soulfully as a *Lightworker*, and that's ultimately what he came to me to find out.

Initially I hadn't a clue on exactly how I was going to go about his reading because I've already had several experiences both in dreams and astral realm. Not many people are educated nor are remotely aware of this realm and I knew that it would be a possible challenge in explaining how I've come to know what I'd seen. But thankfully when Dave and I had spoken on the phone, he added that he's been watching my channel for some time. This was a sure relief and at that point I knew it was a safe move to let Dave be made aware of my experiences. After a few minutes into the session, Dave had mentioned that he had attempted to see another Medium, but she said he wasn't "ready", and she wouldn't let him know anything or even hear from his father's soul.

Whenever I hear this from a client about their previous reading exchange from a fellow Psychic Medium, it tells me one of three possibilities:

1.)
THE MEDIUM MAY NOT LIKE WHAT HE/SHE IS RECEIVING IN INFORMATION AND ISN'T COMFORTABLE IN DELIVERING IT.

2.)
THE MEDIUM DOESN'T KNOW HOW TO HANDLE THE SITUATION WITH DARK SPIRITS AND IS SCARED SO DISMISSES IT ENTIRELY.

3.)
THE PSYCHIC OR MEDIUM DOESN'T SEE ANYTHING AND IS GOING TO TELL THE SITTER (CLIENT) THAT THEY AREN'T "READY", OR THEY AREN'T SEEING ANYTHING AT ALL.

Why would a Psychic Medium tell Dave this? I can understand that maybe it was going to be too difficult for him at the time, and that's why she told Dave to wait on receiving this information -but he HAD to know.

That's the difference with me and most Psychic Mediums is I don't sugar coat the truth. If there's something my client needs to hear that will help them move forward, then I'm going to tell them. Yes, being empathetic in the delivery and being professional is required when being a messenger of the other realms, however this isn't something that is going to reveal itself. Sometimes, you just got to suck it up, and deliver the dose of reality for your client's sake in being made aware of how to prevent something like this happening to them. I'm a firm believer that as a Lightworker and a Psychic Medium I've been dealt the card of transparency and should not only be helping others with healing but also with making them fully aware of the possible dangers that may be lurking in their closets, under their beds or even staring at them in the face. Each time I hear that a Psychic Medium has failed to do so, I have to then make it my mission to see that this person I'm guiding in *Paranormal Advisory* is not only made aware but is given the necessary tools, tips and guidance on how to take care of themselves energetically and Psychicly.

Carefully I delivered the messages to Dave about what happened to his father's soul and what role the demons played. It was apparent both demons were interested in manipulating and influencing Dave's father with alcohol which ultimately became a part of his passing. Despite the fact Dave tried to help his father, it was important for Dave to be made aware that there was nothing that could be done for his father and that it was not his fault. His father was so heavily influenced mentally and Psychicly by the demons manipulating his every move that it was nearly impossible to shake him from the demonic grasp. The only way they could've saved him would've been an exorcism, however even exorcisms like this have been known to kill the possessed person. Heartfelt I was towards the difficult and helpless position Dave was in, but nonetheless, he was not to be blamed, nor should he feel any amount of guilt over the loss on how his dad had died.

Speaking these words from his father's soul was evidence to Dave for it allowed him a peace of mind knowing not only was his father really possessed, more importantly that his father's soul wasn't in hell, nor was he a slave to the demons that killed him.

What got me all shook up was after I had asked Dave this question,...

"Did your father have seizures or something like a seizure? Because my chin kept twitching for days..."

That's when Dave confirmed that before his father's soul departed, he was coughing up blood while twitching similar to like a seizure. In fact, when I had mentioned about the taste of blood Dave's first response was, "Woaahh" He couldn't believe that I even picked that up because the other Medium hadn't detected nor sensed anything relating to his father's soul nor to the connection of his death.

Understandably, Dave's next concern was whether he would have to worry about the demons controlling, influencing or manipulating him the same as his dad. It was a good question! Just the fact that Dave was that focused on remaining in control of himself soulfully and mindfully reassured him as I let him know that the only way demons can manipulate or possess a person to this degree, is if the person gives the entity permission.

Demons and Devil entities can influence us without permission - yes! But they aren't able to fully influence or take over our bodies so much like what his father experienced unless, in this case, there was alcohol involved or drugs. The effects of drugs and alcohol begin to impair the judgment first and it's in losing this ability in one's judgment that can alter one's state of mind towards the Demons and Devil's ability to take possession of the body, mind and even spirit.

Granted there are levels of **HYPNOTISM** that Demons and Devil entities can do to trick humans into doing things, but this isn't as common as most would fear or think.

The fact that Dave was adamant in remaining in control of himself meant Demons would have a hell of a time controlling him even if they tried, which is a very good thing!

SEIZURE INCUBUS

Sometime in September of 2019, I had a request for a *Paranormal Advisory* session from a woman named Elizabeth. It was another video recorded session where I would sit down and tell her what I had previously experienced for the two weeks after scheduling her session. What I had to tell her wasn't pretty, it nearly caused me to completely shut down the whole session entirely after what had happened to me. The experience I had when encountering the demon that entered into my home that was attached to Elizabeth triggered alarm bells to an all-time high. I've come face to face with an exceptional amount of entities now, that it's impossible for me to keep track. But it's not something to take for granted for the threat can be not only emotionally, mentally daunting but can put you in the hospital or in an early grave. These entities **DON'T** mess around and mean business and this demon definitely wanted to make sure I knew that.

During Elizabeth's session I immediately picked up (felt/sensed) the energy of a male spirit and it was negative from the start. That's when Elizabeth admitted to feeling like she was being watched by "something" for a couple of years. Then I asked her these following questions:

ME:
"Do you have panic attacks or anxiety attacks?"

ELIZABETH:
"Oh my god yeah…"

Then I said that the male energy, entity I was seeing and sensing, was very close and watches her like a hawk because it was such an unnerving feeling. Revealing the male spirit was causing all of her anxiety because of his intense focus on her. I was overwhelmed with my own anxiety that this entity was also pushing on me, but I knew I had to continue with the session…

ME:
"Do you ever have nights where it feels like something is laying with you?"

ELIZABETH:
"OH MY GOD!"

Her immediate reaction confirmed the validity of not only what I had been experiencing but what my client had been going through as well. I felt like at this point it was necessary to describe what the entity did to me prior to her session...

ME:
"For several nights I had felt like something was lying next to me or even on top of me while trying to be sexually invasive. My bed was shaking at some points in the middle of the night whenever I felt this entity around me. I also experienced **SLEEP PARALYSIS** on several occasions after scheduling you. All of this happened in the two weeks before our session. But during sleep paralysis, that's when the entity crawled on top of me like a fucking spider. It had a long face, pale, male -very sexual and very creepy. He sexually assaulted me when I was trapped in the paralysis state and there was a point where I was fearful it was trying to possess me…"

After going into describing this uncomfortable detail, that's when I continued the reading by asking further questions that I felt she may had been also experiencing…

ME:

"Do you wake up with bruises on your body that you can't explain?"

ELIZABETH:

"I do, and I did when I was younger, and I do now."

ME:

"I have to ask you a very personal question, but I feel like it's coming up from the reading. Were you ever a victim of sexual assault…?"

ELIZABETH:

"…Yes." She answered tearfully.

I then explained to her that the entity was taking advantage of her emotional vulnerability by using her in this way. By appearing as a male human spirit, but this was a trick. It was trying to trick her, and it was also trying to trick me into thinking it wasn't harmful and that it wasn't a threat -but it was a threat and it certainly *WASN'T* **HUMAN**…

ME:
"I feel like he is trying to choke you when you're sleeping or lying down. I was feeling warm breath on my face at one point. Do you ever experience this?"

ELIZABETH:
"Yes. There are times where I thought I was going crazy because there's no one in my family with this kind of thing happening to them. I thought I could be schizophrenic or losing my mind."

That's when I finally asked the monumental questions…

ME:
"Do you ever wake up shaking uncontrollably from sleep?"

ELIZABETH:
"Yes, sometimes."

ME:
"Do you ever feel like something or someone is poking your forehead, right in between the eyebrows? Poking your head really hard?"

ELIZABETH:
"…Yes?"

This is when I told her of a night terror that shook my literal reality...

ME:
"...What I'm going to tell you is going to be difficult to say but you have to know what I experienced. -The reason why I'm asking you these questions is because it's exactly what I had experienced. There was a night that the same entity had put me into sleep paralysis when I was asleep. Then I could visually see through my third eye -as if my physical eyes were open and watched as this demon crawled on top of me and proceeded to be sexual with me. But the worst part was when it began to open its mouth, then opened mine and then threw up what looked like a black slime-like substance into my mouth. What this did was cause me to go into a violent seizure. My eyes rolled to the back of my head, but I could still see the demon sitting on top of me and my whole body was shaking uncontrollably. I was mumbling words that didn't make sense while at the same time my brain felt like I was being electrocuted. It was one of the most frightening and painful experiences from a demon attack I've ever had."

What shook me even more was after I revealed my experience to Elizabeth, she then admitted that she's been having seizures for a long while and doctors can't find out why she's having them. Not to mention she also was experiencing: chronic fatigue, loss of appetite, sleep paralysis (got that covered!), dizziness, astral attacks, nightmares, physical bruises and moments of rage. But what got me speechless was what she said after I asked her this…

ME:
"Did you ever have a dream or visions where you saw something with long hair, dark and crouched?"

ELIZABETH:
"Actually, that's something I should tell you -it wasn't a dream. I had saw something in my house, in the hallway. It was a dark shadowy figure, with long tangled hair, long nails and crouched on the floor and staring at me."

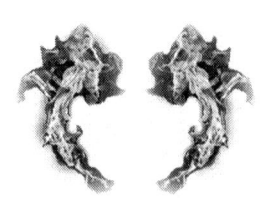

SLEEP PARALYSIS
IS A SHIFT IN CONSCIOUSNESS DURING SLEEP STATE. THE PERSON EXPERIENCES PARANORMAL VISUALS WHILE UNABLE TO MOVE OR SPEAK PHYSICALLY. DOCTORS AND OTHER CLINICAL PROFESSIONS IDENTIFY THE PARANORMAL VISUALS TO BE HALLUCINATIONS FROM THE BRAIN.

THIS IS WHAT THE ENTITY WANTS YOU TO THINK! SLEEP PARALYSIS IS A PSYCHIC ATTACK THAT IS MOST COMMONLY OVERLOOKED AND CAN TURN INTO SERIOUS DANGER IF NOT CONFRONTED IMMEDIATELY!

Not only were my findings correct and validating for Elizabeth to know she wasn't crazy, but it too gave me reassurance that I also wasn't losing my sanity.

The issue most often when people attempt to be open about their paranormal experiences, is they get judged and are advised to see a doctor for their 'hallucinations'. Granted, if my client had a history of experimenting with illegal drugs then I'd usually advise the person that they may be experiencing paranormal phenomenon but that they should still see their doctor. I'm not a doctor and have no right nor the legal ability to diagnose nor give advice on what a person should do medically. I am not legally allowed to do that nor should I. It wouldn't be serving the client with the best care possible.

In Elizabeth's case I knew she wasn't using narcotics or illegal drugs that may have caused her experiences. Not to forget the undeniable connection between her experiences and my own that is nearly impossible to ever happen *twice* especially in the two weeks of me scheduling her. She never once mentioned anything to me in email, text or on the phone that she had been experiencing seizures. Nor has she mentioned in the slightest detail of the entity in her home. This was our first and only phone call and detailed conversation about her experiences and it was evident enough to say the least that we both knew she was in serious danger.

There was no denying that Elizabeth was under **DEMONIC OPPRESSION** for a few years. In fact, her session became such an inspiration to me due to how bizarre my experience as a Psychic Medium was that I decided to draw the entity. Hoping that if she saw what I saw, that it would further validate my findings and more importantly her paranormal haunting. When I finally got done with drawing the entity and showed it to Elizabeth, she couldn't help but express how much it not only looked like it, but gave her a sense of further reassurance that she wasn't losing her sense of reality.

DEMON DEALER

MELINDA KAY LYONS

CRISTINA'S DEMON MASSACRE

Since the experience from Elizabeth's case, my awareness has been sharpened. Each and every case is another test of my Psychic muscles and after each unique malevolent confrontation, I learn more and become stronger.

There's a saying that the more a fighter goes into a ring and either loses or wins always comes out stronger, wiser and more prepared than the last fight. That's how I look at each demonic encounter when helping my clients. It doesn't tempt the urge to quit, rather to keep pushing forward with each stride in hope, will and determination that no matter what, I not only will overcome it, but will build further enlightenment for others likeminded. In Cristina's case, it was the kind of paranormal plunge that continues to encourage the motion towards this example.

Cristina is a single mom of two young sons, one being autistic. She requested my help sometime in October 2019, to give her some clarity on the weird paranormal activity that was occurring in her home and that was affecting her sons.

In my website when requesting a session with me in *Paranormal Advisory*, I let people mention a few select things that's been happening and why they need my help. It's important that I at least know a few things of the person's experiences so as to understand their level of threat. But I still request that the client not put in too much leading information that could otherwise negatively influence the reading experience. Though it's free and doesn't cost my client a dime, it's still important to me that the clients receive as much validation as possible in their reading. When she contacted me, she did mention a few things including a story from her words that I'd like to share with you now. It not only was disturbing but it led me to believe that there was much more going on with her than she may have realized…

Melinda Kay Lyons

CRISTINA:

Cristina's Case: Cross 2019

"I just had noticed my mom's ashes that have been sitting up on a shelf since she passed away in 2011 were missing. I don't know what made me even look and notice that it was gone, but it wasn't there. I began freaking out wondering what was going on because it was in the middle of all of the paranormal activity we've been having. I came to find her ashes were in my son's room just thrown in the closet. I couldn't understand why he would do that, but he has a hard time communicating because he is autistic. I kept asking him if he did it and he then told me he did do it, but he couldn't tell me why. He said he didn't know why he did it, why he put it in there. So, I found that really, really odd…I have a cross, that actually happened the day or so before the ashes incident. I had a cross that was sitting in the windowsill by my bed because all of this was going on. The night before I got very sick to my stomach, I was nauseous, had a headache and was freezing no matter what I did. I was also very exhausted, so I decided to go to bed. When I was trying to sleep, I had sleep paralysis. The next day, I woke up and still didn't feel right and I noticed the cross I had sitting by my bed in the windowsill was broken in three pieces. It hadn't fallen on the floor, nothing that I could see or explain physically. That really scared me. Then I got a call from my eleven-year old son's school, and they said that he was having an anxiety attack. The anxiety attack was happening on the same day when I discovered my cross like this."

Of course, when I read her story it intrigued me greatly. I've never heard of such a story like hers before. However, I knew that scheduling her would mean the entity that may have been haunting her and her two sons, wouldn't shy from my abilities, or my purpose. Not only was this spirit not shy, it appeared to me in a dream rather quickly and made sure without any exceptions that it wasn't going to go down without a fight.

It appeared one night in a dream, and in this dream, I found myself walking alone in an alley somewhere and it was dark out. I remember specifically seeing a red light in the alley that was blinking on and off every few seconds in a slow motion. As I was walking, I then see a man that looked similar to my Twin Flame. But when he approached me it was clear to see he wasn't my Twin Flame and said in a deep, disturbing voice...

"I'M GUNA KILL YOU."

Instinctively I tried to run away from him and came up to a ladder with a pole and attempted to climb it that led towards a fence. However, the man was so fast that he pulled me down and then revealed a knife from his pocket. Just before he was going to stab me, I took the knife from his grasp and jabbed it into one of his eyes. He smiled while pulling the knife from his flesh saying, **"OH REALLY, YOU LIKE PAIN..."** And in this instance, he proceeded to stab me in the chest, stomach and then slowly sliced my throat. As the knife slid across my throat, I could feel blood oozing from my inside of my body and spilling on my shirt and hands as I tried to stop the bleeding. The more I bled, the more faint I became and at the same time felt a large sense of warmth overtake me as my body gently made to the ground.

Not a few seconds later, my Spirit Guides, including Angels, Joshua (Yehoshua), my Twin Flame came to my rescue. They made it a point to apprehend the demon by restraining him while Joshua (Yehoshua/ Jesus) helped me to remember it was just an illusion.

What a lot of victims of demonic dreams don't know is these nightmares can become so real to the person that it can feel as if it happened to your mortal physical self. The demon wants it to feel real because if the nightmare is *that* convincing, it can cause the brain activity and heart to suddenly stop. If I wasn't made aware of this reminder, I could've easily died in my sleep. I was nearly convinced that my throat really was cut open and I was meeting with death. Once I collected myself mentally in the dream -which now I know was the astral realm, I confronted the demon and spoke to it. And what it told me was it wasn't going to leave Cristina's family and wasn't going to be stopped, but...

HE HASN'T MET ME

My Spirit Guides come to my rescue much more than I'd like to admit but I'm always forever appreciative and grateful for their generous time and care in ensuring my mortal safety. It's nothing to be ashamed of even as a Demonologist. For it doesn't matter how long one has been faced with evil, you'll always need help from your team, and that's who they are to me. They guide me, assure me, love and assist me with further knowledge, wisdom while reminding me that it's okay to also get angry and kick astral ass when it's necessary. (That's information that will be heavily shared in a later Chapter). No one is perfect nor truly invincible and will always find they have to seek assistance from others. Even Angels help each other in battle, so it shouldn't be a surprise for a Demonologist, Exorcist, Priest, Shaman, Reiki Master or even a Psychic Medium to need the same ethereal support.

After I woke up from the nightmare, I could feel my entire room was freezing cold. Though in Alaska its winter a large portion of the year, the heat in the house is fairly warm and doesn't typically become ice cold. But in this room that night, it might as well have been considered a large walk-in freezer.

Not to sound morbid, but though these experiences are considered controversial and malicious, it's the deeper and personal experiences that give me another perspective on how spirits like demons haunt. I don't like these nightmares or the horror that follows in my career, but I can't help to admit, that whenever I have these types of metaphysical confrontations, it entices more interest in continuing my work. And by the time Cristina and I had her session, I can confess I was kind of excited to reveal the nightmare and the information I received...

ME:

"Now before we begin, I need to tell you that what I experienced in the two weeks before your session was alarming. Because nearly every night I've had nightmares, astral attacks, smelling fowl smells like rotten eggs or rotten meat, tasting blood and have gotten continual stabbing pains in my head. -But, do you sometimes also slip memory? Something could be recent, but you sometimes draw a blank. Does this happen?"

CRISTINA:

"Yes, it does happen."

ME:
"Yehoshua has been very close with me for your session. That's almost never. That's how serious your situation is, because of the severity and how old this entity is. Though this spirit seems young, and hip -as weird as that sounds. The entity that I have been seeing has short black hair, he almost looks Asian, or another type of race. His eyes are black but at the same time he seems Caucasian. He seems all smoky and this is his natural demonic form. He looks like his own storm, surrounded in smoke and ash as his natural form. He shapes himself as a person but that's his way of trying to trick me or anyone that possibly sees him…"

CRISTINA:
"I do feel like whatever it is, comes to me as people that I know are passed away. I feel like he disguises himself by trying to make me feel comfortable with him and to think that it's not something negative, but I always can feel that its negative."

ME:
"Have you been hearing a man's voice in your home when no one else is around?"

CRISTINA:

"I have at various times. Its more so at night most of it is when I'm trying to go to sleep at night, but it has happened another time."

ME:

"Are you ever feeling pinches at the back of your neck?"

CRISTINA:

"Yes."

This is when I began to pick up that she was researching demonology and she too confirmed she's been looking into it and it was how she found me...

ME:

"Have you been having or finding scratch marks on the walls or on your skin?"

CRISTINA:

"On me, I have."

ME:

"Do you feel as if someone is lying down with you as you sleep at night?"

CRISTINA:
"I have at times. Not so much recently but I have felt that."

ME:
"Do you experience paranormal activity? Like doors opening and closing, things moving…?"

CRISTINA:
"Um yes. Doors definitely opening and closing for sure."

Eventually I learned from the reading and after speaking with my guides that her session wasn't about getting rid of the entity. It was about helping her and teaching on how to get rid of it herself through self-empowerment tips and demonology guidance. This type of session isn't for all cases and is only necessary when I've established through enough evidence and Psychic experience that I feel the client is Psychicly able through also being a Lightworker themselves.

Cristina and her sons are all *sensitives* and it was becoming more professionally clear that her family were being targeted for a reason. This doesn't mean I didn't help her with getting rid of the entity, however I instructed her divine ability in ceasing the situation on her own with enough practice, meditation and self-confidence energetically and soulfully…

CRISTINA:

"That's exactly what I've been trying to do because I don't want to put up with it anymore. Yeah, everything you're saying makes sense to me."

I sensed and later uncovered Cristina was struggling with self-confidence and a sense of security in herself. She then admitted that she was fearful in meditation because she was afraid of what she might see or find. But due to this, she felt that she may have put up a Psychic wall.

Here, I soon explained to her how both of her sons and her are open to spirit and are all sensitives. But her son that's autistic (Gabriel) is a natural target for spiritual influence, to the point where he could become easily possessed without any warning. This can happen because of being more in-tune with spirits without even realizing it. People with mental disabilities tend to have a bright light inside of them which can make them a prime target for demonic influence and familiar negative spirits.

Since Cristina's session, she's reported that most of the activity have ceased and more importantly she's been working on herself through meditation. Whenever there's a serious case like Cristina's I like to take time on the astral realm to return to her home to check and see how things are going.

What I clearly remember was when I was there with Yehoshua, he showed me where the demon liked to stay in the closet, which also was the same place where Cristina's mother's ashes were placed from her son, Gabriel. Thankfully with the help of Angels and Yehoshua the attachment has been cut, and the entity was banished out of her home on the astral realm.

Can the entity return? Yes! Which is why building Cristina's Psychic abilities and self-reliance through confidence building is crucial in order to sustain the astral peace. However, this type of training takes much time, focus and patience without judgement on one's self.

It won't be quiet all of her life because she is a Psychic Medium and will always be the light attracting dark entities. But that doesn't mean she should give in to the otherworldly beasts. Gaining control in herself and in her home will be a daily battle her whole life. This is true for all those that are guiding lights to the other side and is a part of the curse with the blessing as an awakened person.

A few weeks later, I received a message on Instagram from Cristina informing me of her son's encounter of the same demon that I described to her. Below is the copy of that message. Not only did her son describe the entity exactly the same way as I did but Cristina agreed that the demon that I drew looked similar to the one they have both seen.

In my drawing of this demon, the intent was to articulate the Demon's anger towards my client's family and against anyone who charges against him.

Demons are metaphysical beings that were never human but will make themselves **APPEAR** as humans in order to gain the person's trust through deception. It's absolutely critical in establishing the understanding that demons no matter how human they appear -**ARE NOT AND NEVER WERE.**

DEMON DEALER

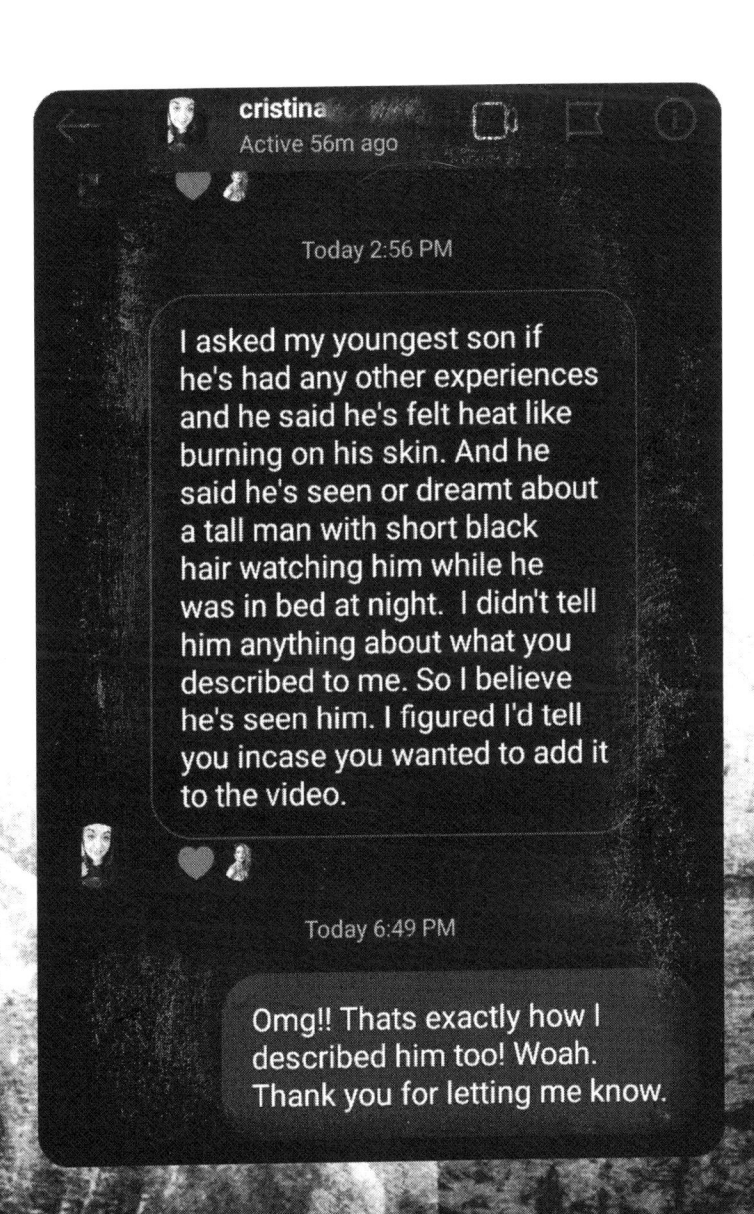

cristina
Active 56m ago

Today 2:56 PM

I asked my youngest son if he's had any other experiences and he said he's felt heat like burning on his skin. And he said he's seen or dreamt about a tall man with short black hair watching him while he was in bed at night. I didn't tell him anything about what you described to me. So I believe he's seen him. I figured I'd tell you incase you wanted to add it to the video.

Today 6:49 PM

Omg!! Thats exactly how I described him too! Woah. Thank you for letting me know.

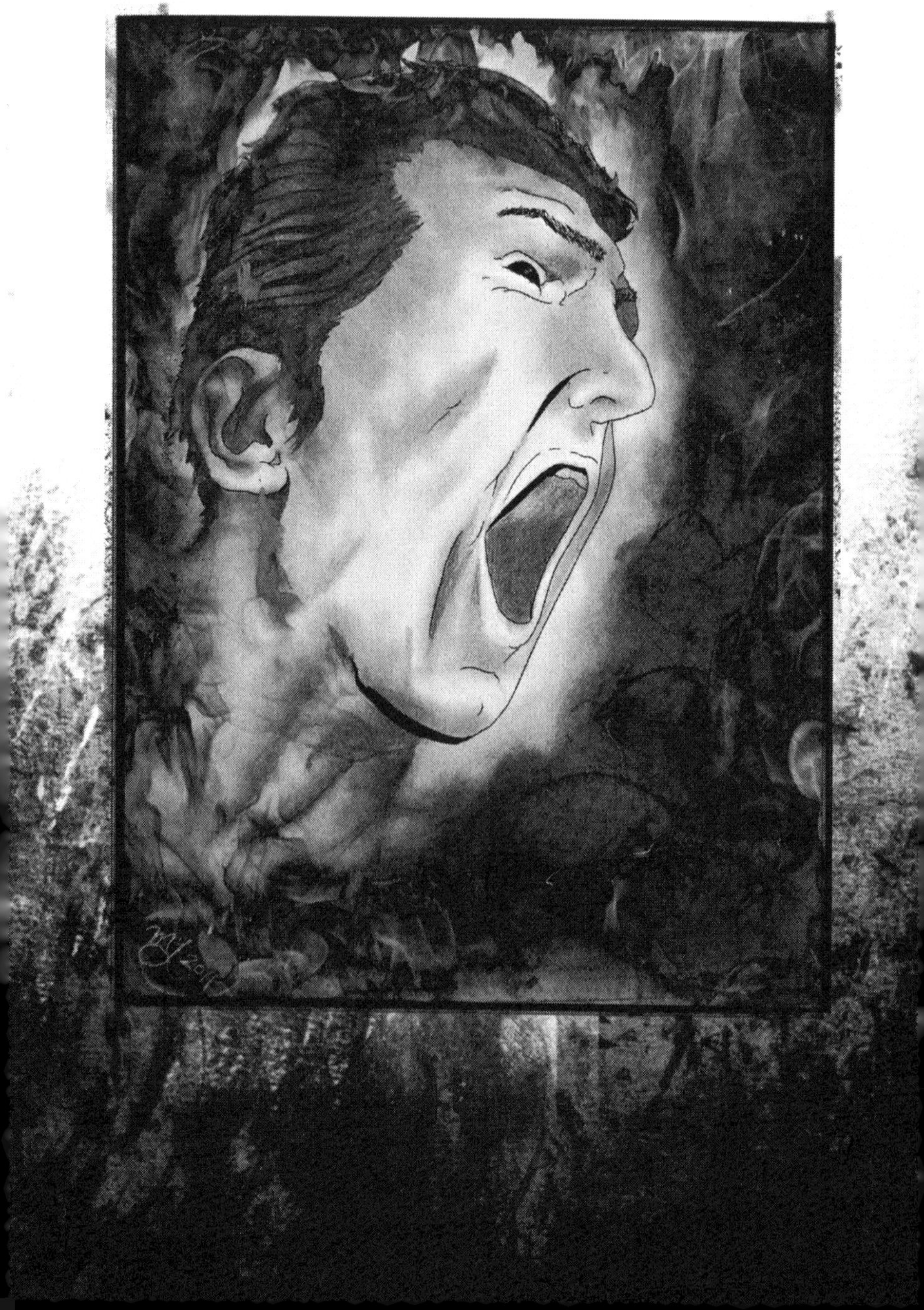

PARANORMAL ADVISORY AFTERMATH

Each case is unique and so are the entities in them. Some cases are emotionally, mentally, psychicly and physically draining and will require me to have much needed rest afterward. Then there are some cases where it doesn't drain me at all and was a walk in the park -not in a dark alley.

I've made the conscious decision after many of my own frightening experiences to make it my soul mission to help others from their own metaphysical terrors. But it's not smooth in all cases at times because every few there will be that one case where the client desperately seeks my help but then doesn't take any of my advice. This happens. It's a lot like that saying, "You can lead a horse to water, but you can't make him drink." Even though they took the time to express on every level of their haunting experience, then I'll find the person just isn't satisfied with my professional advice and will politely decline.

Then there's the graceful types that will insult my abilities and won't take any of my advice and claim "god will take care of them." Which I always find humorous because if that's their whole-hearted belief, then why waste my time trying to help you in the first place? Considering it's against Christianity to seek help from a Psychic Medium -let alone speak to one. But I let it go and allow my focus to be on those that trust in what I've devoted into their preternatural invasion with gratitude and appreciation.

No matter how the case ends, whether its successful or not, the ultimate goal is to make the person aware and to get answers in their situation.

Whenever I receive *Paranormal Advisory* letter requests, I know it's never easy for someone to admit they may be haunted, or someone who's just heard of me and of my work. But I take each letter very seriously and answer the select few I feel *Psychicly* are the most prone to a demonical or preternatural surrender of the otherworldly threats. It's what I'm passionate about and it's what drives me to live another day.

Unveiling the energy in each case creates much turmoil in my own home but if it gives a person answers, validation and reassurance that they aren't crazy -then I'll keep answering letters and continue doing it until the day I die.

DEMON DEALER

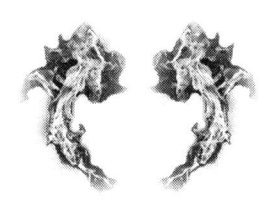

What you are about to read
are personal experiences with some of the
worst negative spirits
I've ever encountered.

Due to the severity of the rest of the following
content, one may experience severe triggering
moments. Reader's discretion is advised!!

In order for me to write the following,
I was heavily guarded by angels, and
Ascended Master Yehoshua.

The entities mentioned are real and know
you are reading this now!!

It's highly advisable to protect oneself with
prayer and other chosen methods before
proceeding!!

MELINDA KAY LYONS

BASED ON A TRUE STORY

BOOKS

One of the major impacts after my energetic and soulful ascensions, is the ability to see and do way more than anticipated. One of the issues through being able to walk between two worlds is the art of not just sensing -but seeing nearly everything. It started happening after my soul had ascended to the fifth dimension of consciousness. When a person **ASCENDS**, they are gifted further abilities from **LORDS OF THE UNIVERSE**. This is how I like to identify them, or one may call them **ASCENDED MASTERS**. Through different levels of personal trials, and sacrifices in my Psychic Mediumship and Demonology journey, they gifted me with further agility and ability in order to see, hear and sense entities better on other dimensions.

Life in the demonology field brings upon the individual a lifetime supply of horror accompanied by uninvited metaphysical visitors. Each time a negatively charged spirit shows up at my home my crown chakra will begin ringing with warning signals as my Psychic abilities begin to read the astral intruder that's lurking in the shadows. The upper hand in being a Demonologist, is that I'm also a Psychic Medium.

Most Demonologists are not Psychicly aware nor are they astral experts in order to see the spirits or their abilities. This is what makes me different. Excitedly there's been more Psychic Mediums that I know of that are actively pursuing Demonology to have greater chances at success in helping their clients and themselves. But realistically, there's still a larger scale of demons haunting and harming innocent people than there are those that are brave enough to face them. Doing this type of work doesn't make one a hero, but what it does do is greater your chances at making malevolent enemies.

I can't even watch or read anything paranormal that's *"based on a true story"* in books or in film without being astrally and Psychicly prepared. Due to demons, familiar evil spirits or devil entities that are based on the stories in history -famous or not, they arrive at my home nearly each time. It's been a title wave from this reality to such a degree that it's caused me to be even more guarded on what I spend my time watching or reading. The moment this started to really happen was when I began to notice that books I'd read about people in history, or based on demonology, the souls from the subject matter that died would show up at my home. Some have said that it's because I'm attracting them to my home and so that makes it my fault. However, what I've come to uncover after lucid conversations with these spirits, is they not only have heard of me but wanted me to know they existed. Sometimes the spirit will arrive in hopes to convince me to turn me evil through temptation such as: power, control over entities, lust of money, fame, greed, sex etc.

As tantalizing as those temptations can be to the ego, it's just not worth it because the entity always turns on you and makes you their slave -I know this from personal experience. Other times the entity will appear in determination to frighten me from my mission and use fear, pain and manipulative maneuvers to scare me "normal".

MELINDA KAY LYONS

ADOLF HITLER

Sometime in 2018 I was going through books to read in *Barnes & Noble* (of course one of my favorite stores). As I was searching through the *New Age* section of books and gazing past some of the famous authors and inspirations, I heard the name "HITLER" in my head loud and clear. Not sure if this was possibly the universe giving me an idea of what else to venture upon, I decided to trust in this information and allowed the energy pull to lead the way. As soon as I reached to the "Biography" section, I came across Adolf Hitler titles and chose one to purchase.

What people don't know about me is I'm actually a fanatic about history. Honestly, that still surprises me because in my younger years I never cared much for history, but there was always something about the diabolical nature of evil people in history that fascinated me. Don't get it twisted -I'm not in support of Hitler or anyone like him in that way! In fact, in my Freshmen year of high school, we were given the chance to do a history essay on whatever we wanted in my English class. My paper was based on the Holocaust and how much humanity suffered from this great terrorist of a man and his allies. Little did I know that the reason I was triggered by these types of historical tragedies, was because of my humanitarianism, empathic abilities and my Lightworker code.

None of it made sense when I wrote the essay or when I even purchased this book years later, but I knew that I wanted to get into Hitler's mind and see how he thought, why he thought it, and how he became the monster that he was. I figured that maybe reading and learning more about him as a human being, would allow me the chance at understanding the basic level of malevolence and where it starts and how someday we could possibly prevent it.

During my reading on Hitler, I couldn't help but slightly pity the guy because of how he was raised and how he never seemed to get what was fair to him. This sympathy or empathy wasn't to suggest I was suddenly supporting what he did to millions of innocent people - but it did start to explain to me why and how his mindset shaped his thoughts.

What I've learned the most from Yehoshua, is each person does something for a reason, and not always for the reasons we immediately assume. And most often, it may even be for reasons that specific person isn't remotely aware of. I'm no psychologist nor a therapist, so I obviously won't and can't say exactly why Adolf became the monster he was, but what I can tell you is that when my empathic side grew - ***HE DAMN WELL KNEW IT.***

Adolf didn't seem to want to waste any time when he learned I was reading about him. Within a few chapters of reading and those feelings of pity developed ***(very, very small amount)*** that intrigued him. So much so, that he trapped me in a dream state that I'll never forget.

In this dream, I found myself with other souls, including one of my most trusted and loving spirit guides, Hunter. He's been with me for many difficult situations and has helped me heal and learn to love myself through many trials. Seeing Hunter at this time in the dream was very typical for me and I knew I was safe with him. We were romantically involved for a long while, nearly a year when I think on it now…

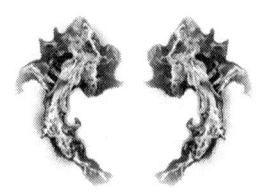

*Yes, you can have relationships with spirits,
and it has been one of the most rewarding experiences of my life.
Hunter has helped me more than I can count.
It's thanks to him I work on loving myself each day and that's
something I'll forever be grateful for.* ♥

Being in this dream, I was surrounded by loving positive souls with Hunter, and we were just having a good time laughing, dancing and talking to one another. But then out of nowhere, Hunter notices a change in his energy, and motioned to me that we immediately had to leave but we were too late. Suddenly, a large group of men circulated around all of us. There must've been at least thirty men and the leader to appear from the massive threat was Hitler. Hunter kept me behind him to protect me, and we uncomfortably watched as many of the men began to hurt the innocent souls around us. It didn't take Adolf long to begin threatening everyone with harm if we didn't abide by his one demand, and what he wanted was me. Of course, Hunter denied his demand.

Angrily in a quick swoop, Adolf grabbed another woman I didn't know and said he would allow his men to hurt her in any way they pleased if I didn't go with them.

The fear in her eyes was unbearable. I couldn't let something happen to another innocent person on account of me. In fact, this girl seemed so youthful that I soon understood this woman was a teenager. She begged to be set free but the greedy smiles full of sin on the men's faces only widened in excitement. You could easily view the horrifying imagination manifesting in their minds as the moments passed ever so slowly. My heart couldn't take it anymore and it was then I stepped forward and said to Hitler…

ME:

"Why do you want *her??* -Look at her…she's too young for you anyway… Don't you want a woman who knows what she's doing? … and can do… it… **right**."

In saying this I had manifested myself into lingerie to persuade the thirst for their desire of control, fear and power.

Hitler's expression not only revealed to everyone he was interested in my offer but that his ego from his previous life hadn't changed a bit. And in that, the exchange was made. They threw the young frightful female to the ground as I walked to one of the most hated and feared men in the world and in human history. I couldn't believe this was actually happening and when I looked at the man I loved, who's protected and cared for me for what felt like forever, the pain and fear in his eyes made it all too factual.

The connection we have is strong, that we're able to sense what the other soul is thinking. He knew I didn't want to go and he knew all too well what would happen to me if I did. Then it was in this instance he fought for me and for the others.

Unable to prevent the outrage the large group of men surrounding the innocent became a war zone of good vs. evil. Angels and demons joined as we all were in the middle of this astral fight for one's freedom against the Hitler party. One hit, one strike after the other was loud, bloody and unapologetic to the targeted enemy. Angels did the best they could but the more demons that had appeared the harder it became for them to protect everyone. And before I could even know where it would end, the men that held me captive took me though I fought as best as I could.

Although I've ascended, there's still the reality that no one is truly undefeated. I may have ascended to learn how to battle and fight demons and help people but there's always going to be tricks up spirit's sleeves that will make you vulnerable to their trickery.

And it was in this moment where about seven of them were carrying me to what appeared to be a portal that Hitler ordered to be opened. When the portal was fully exposed, the men forced me on my knees as I could still hear the screams and holler of the war around me while facing Adolf's hideous pleasure. Unable to escape, they pinned me heavily on the floor unable to move. Feeling as if I'd suddenly become a thousand pounds of heavy that couldn't be lifted unless by the Gods of mercy. It wasn't the crowd they were interested in, it was me and without knowing it, gave them exactly what Hitler wanted. Scared both, physically and soulfully, for I didn't know what was going to happen, but I knew that I had to remain calm. I didn't want him to see my fear as much as I could help or conceal it. But no matter how much I tried to hide my fear, they could see it, they could see it well.

I still remember one of the men's faces looking down at me and all I could see was pain, suffering, with a dash of hell in the shadowed sockets where eyes should've been. The longer I stared, it was evident the men in alliance of Hitler were not that different from demons. The energy permeating from the soldiers of darkness were equipped with humor and delight from the heart-stricken fear that was growing inside of me by the seconds. Amused they were by the screams of terror streaming along their sight and sound, and they wanted more of it. These are souls that have descended towards the depths of anguish too uncomfortable that even they can be mistaken as an unclean spirit if chosen to appear so.

After Adolf had exchanged conversation with his fellow followers in a quieted confidence of what he was planning next, he then spoke to me directly.

ADOLF HITLER:
"DO YOU KNOW WHY I'VE BROUGHT YOU HERE MELINDA?"

ME:
"…No. Except that maybe because I've been reading about you?"

ADOLF HITLER:
"…I AM AWARE OF YOU READING ABOUT ME BUT THAT IS NOT WHY I'VE BROUGHT YOU HERE -BUT SINCE YOU BROUGHT IT UP, WHAT DID YOU THINK OF MY LITTLE BACKSTORY MELINDA?"

While not looking at me, Hitler walked to a small vintage bar and made himself a glass of what appeared to be a shot of his favorite alcohol. Savoring the taste as he listened to my shaken response...

Me:
"...Sad."

Adolf Hitler:
"I see. So, you pity me is that it?"

Me:
"No but I can see now why you chose your path. What you did was horrible and wrong to millions of people that never deserved what happened to them -but it still slightly explains your reason for such madness."

Adolf Hitler:
"I see. Most people don't understand my vision for the better world, a world that is without imperfections -including the type of humans in it. I thought you were a smart woman, but you are just as naïve as the rest of the fools I've encountered..."

Looking at his glass of possibly whiskey, he filled it a second time, swirled the shiny liquid of intoxication and continued…

ADOLF HITLER:
"…You see Melinda, I was trying to make a world much like how this was made -perfect. Shaping the taste and it's ingredients by taking away and adding something new. I thought that life after death was possible, but I didn't ever know just how powerful one can be. Which is why I absolutely love being here in this moment now. The energy, the power, the freedom I have here is better than one could ever expect and more. Why would I ever want to go back to the same pathetic world you call earth? It's dry, lifeless and full of puny people with nothing going for them. They all deserve to suffer in order to learn of their rightful place."

ME:
"I will admit that this realm is far more exciting and exhilarating than anything I've ever imagined. I do love it here and there's days where I hate being on earth. -But you're wrong Adolf. The people on earth are good people that are simply trying to learn how to survive and

how to cope with the negativity that surrounds them. The suffering is brought on by themselves and that is also stimulated from others and from situations. And no matter how insignificant they may seem to you, I love them because they are trying to love themselves and better themselves. You're right. There are many people on earth right now, wasting their lives on alcohol, drugs, addictions, and through other pointless pursuits that will never truly serve them in the long run. But each person -each soul learns from their living experiences as I did and as they grow from their suffering they slowly evolve into better people with a hope for a brighter future. And as for perfection -it's folly to seek for something that doesn't exist. Perfection is in the eye of the beholder, just like beauty. No idea of perfection is right nor wrong but based on one's own perception such as your own. But the perfection you seek is nothing but a shallow expectation that will eventually fail. I won't deny that I care even for you as a person but what you've done to so many innocent people will never go unnoticed nor forgotten. Imperfections is what make us all unique. Just like a rose that has only a slight discoloration compared to the others, doesn't make it less beautiful, only different. Imperfections aren't bad, just different and that is what creates a better world. A world full of unique souls with different dreams and ideas, goals and love. No one is perfect, not even me, no matter where I've come from. But I care for them and that will never change."

ADOLF HITLER:
"...Hmm. They said you were a strong humanitarian, but now I see what they mean on how much power you have."

ME:
"What power? - Who's *they*? Who said this?"

ADOLF HITLER:
"Let's just say I have friends in low places that would pay me a high reward for turning you in to them."

ME:
"I don't know what or why you and your "*friends*" would care so much about me. But I swear to you I'm nothing but another person just trying to help people find a positive side to themselves. I've not done anything to you or to anyone, I'm just trying to help people. I'm nothing special and you're wasting your time."

Triggered, his eyes now connect with mine and it was here I wish I didn't say anything else. But he continued calmly like a businessman making a deal...

ADOLF HITLER:
"OH MELINDA, MELINDA... YOU'RE LYING TO YOURSELF AND YOU KNOW IT. YOU MUST KNOW BY NOW ON JUST HOW SPECIAL YOU ARE. HAVEN'T YOU HEARD IT? THE WHISPERS FROM WHAT EVERYONE HAS BEEN SAYING?... YOU'RE THE NEXT WOMAN TO REUNITE THE NEXT LEVEL OF CONSCIOUSNESS TO HUMANITY. YOU'RE THE THREAT THAT EVEN LUCIFER WOULD DO ANYTHING FOR HIM TO HAVE. THINK ON IT KID, HAVEN'T YOU EVER FELT A DIFFERENT SIDE OF YOURSELF THAT MAKES YOU FEEL LIKE YOU DON'T BELONG ON EARTH...?"

The more he was talking the more I could hear a voice inside of me that never said a word, but I knew exactly what he was saying. In a strange way the thoughts inside of myself were starting to connect to a deeper level of awareness that were being confirmed by this monster's words. And the more he stared at me the more he could see I was starting to believe it...

ADOLF HITLER:
"...A HUH... YOU DO KNOW OF WHAT I SPEAK. YOU HAVE KNOWN THIS ALL ALONG. BUT YOU'RE MORE POWERFUL THAN THESE PATHETIC HUMANS, WHY WOULD YOU WANT

TO WASTE ALL OF THAT POWER ON SUCH A DISGUSTING WASTE OF LIFE?"

ME:

"I can't deny I've always felt… like I was different. But I don't know exactly what it means or how different I am. Yes. I do feel like I don't truly belong on earth. It's always felt like I've come from somewhere else. But I'm no better than them. I've made plenty of mistakes and have done many things I regret and wish I could take back, but yes… even to you I cannot lie I've felt this vibration inside that is meant for…so much more."

Hitler's eyes could not only see but sensed I was being truthful. It was in his motions of his energy that I could also feel he wasn't as aggressive in this moment and continued…

ADOLF HITLER:

"MELINDA, THIS IS EXACTLY WHY YOU MUST BE STOPPED BEFORE YOU GET BETTER. YOU'RE A COMMODITY THAT HAS TO BE PRESERVED AND IN THE RIGHT HANDS. YOU'RE THE TYPE OF WEAPON WE WANT ON OUR TEAM, AND AS SOON AS YOU GET YOUR CROWN, YOU'RE GOING TO BE NEARLY UNSTOPPABLE AND THAT MAKES YOU VERY DESIRABLE IN THE WEAPONRY DEPARTMENT."

Adolf took a seat that magically appeared before my very eyes. It was red with a soft cloth I've never seen before on earth that shimmered and gleamed with carvings engraved in his seat of evil. Though he sat amused like a royal king taking a rest as he lingered the talk in cosmic detail, also stared at my legs still fastened to the floor...

ME:

"*Crown...?* What do you mean *crown*? I don't have anything like that. - And I'm no weapon dude, did you not easily just detain me now? How much of a threat am I *seriously??*"

ADOLF HITLER:

"-TRUE. YOU WERE EASY TO ACCESS INTO OUR CUSTODY BUT THAT'S WHY WE DECIDED TO ACT ON THIS NOW FOR WITHIN A MATTER OF MONTHS YOU'RE GOING TO BE ONE OF THE MOST STELLAR FORCES THE UNIVERSE HAS EVER SEEN. AND THAT'S WHY YOU'RE HERE. WE WANT YOU TO BE ABLE TO HAVE ALL OF THE POWER YOU COULD EVER WANT AND MORE AND YOU COULD BE CAPABLE OF ANYTHING AND EVERYTHING YOU COULD EVER DESIRE. WE WILL NEVER STOP YOU, DETAIN YOU OR GET IN YOUR WAY EVER AGAIN..."

ME:
"-Wait. Are you trying to make a **DEAL** with me? You want me to work for you, don't you?"

ADOLF HITLER:
"THINK OF IT MORE AS A TRUCE. WE WON'T BOTHER YOU AND YOU WON'T BOTHER US. THAT'S WHAT WE WANT.
-YOU CAN HAVE OUR ARMIES WORK IN YOUR COMMAND AND BE A PART OF YOUR LEVERAGE AS MUCH AS YOU COULD POSSIBLY DESIRE... MELINDA. YOU COULD BE THE CROWNED GODDESS OF ALL TIME. EVERYONE WOULD OBEY YOUR EVERY COMMAND."

The more I listened to his "truce" the more suspicious it became. None of the crown talk made sense to me (at the moment) and it was becoming clear of what this was all about.

There's a common understanding in Psychic Mediumship that after a course of time, one begins to experience special **ASCENSION TESTS** of one's loyalty and of their ability to look past ego. Sometimes these tests can be so brutal based on the rawness of just how desperate one can behave if triggered by the right type of desire. And it was here, in this moment, on the floor and whether it was purposeful or not, felt like one of those tests...

ME:
"Why do I feel like this is a test…? Is this another Ascension Test?"

Hitler looked at me and bellowed a laugh and replied…

ADOLF HITLER:
"NO, THIS IS NOT A TEST. THIS IS VERY REAL AND I'M DELIVERING THIS MESSAGE DIRECTLY FROM LUCIFER IF YOU MUST KNOW. THIS OFFER OF TRUCE IS ONLY OFFERED NOW AND WILL NOT BE OPENED LONG. IF YOU'D LIKE A SIGHT OF WHAT IT WOULD BE LIKE, I CAN HAVE ONE OF MY MEN SHOW YOU. WOULD YOU LIKE TO SEE? I KNOW YOU'RE AT LEAST A BIT CURIOUS…"

ME:
"…I would like to see but only as long as Hunter is here with me. I want to make sure he's safe. And the others. I won't consider your offer unless you guarantee you'll let them go and leave everyone alone right now. Only then, will I take a look to see through curiosity."

His smile widened and without a word he tilted his head back in his red engraved seat and sent out a telepathic order to his devilish champions to retreat. Within seconds all the war had stopped, and his jaded followers vanished in dust leaving the rest of the people unharmed. Quickly the Angels were aware of the negotiation and guided the rest of the souls out of the realm to safety. Hunter was then taken and forced by my side by two of Hitler's dedicated soldiers. Once Hunter and I exchanged looks, the vision of sight had already begun.

Inside my mind I began swirling into a vortex of different levels of moments watching as exactly what Adolf said I'd become. I had seen that my abilities were not only much more advanced but that I could shapeshift while wearing the crown on my head similar to like a tiara. The crown was unlike one would see in films, on a bright stage or in a costume shop. It was made of special materials that are only known to the Ascended Realms.

It gleamed, capturing a light that could not only guide others but granted me immense abilities beyond my wildest dreams. Jewels were imbedded safely in the detail of the majestic tiara of ability. A mere glance of another in my crown gave demons fright for it signified the power of Ascended nobility. I can still remember flying above the ground as I could feel the energy surge within every part of me unwaveringly. My skin glowed and shined similar to the many specks of sand sparkling from the sun's ray during a hot summer day. Every part of me felt charged and ready for anything. I loved it. It was as how I've always imagined my soul could become in each motion I conjured. Not without too appreciating the whimsical long locks of hair that changed color by mere thought.

I could feel others cower over as I walked through the valley of shadows. Demons ran from my presence to escape the light from inside of me that draped over the darkness. One demon as tall as ten feet stood before me in reluctant obedience and bowed down before me then the rest of the demons followed in likeness.

As the league of demons bowed, Adolf's voice spoke in a chant like taunt reassuring me that I'd have all of the power in myself to control everyone, and everything by a mere thought in my mind. That I could defeat any entity even faster if I just had his truce. His echo was soft at first, but over the course of a few seconds aggression ravaged his patience and soon my mind…

Adolf Hitler:
"…You can have your own league of demons that worship and follow you. You will become the leading Demon Goddess that's forever worshipped and feared by many. You can have as many legions of demons as you so desire…"

Me:
"I could be that powerful…?"

Adolf Hitler:
"Without a doubt... As powerful as even Lucifer himself if you wanted. And you would never be denied anything. You can have anything and everything you've ever desired..."

I can't deny the lust for power was all too alluring. Everything he said was overwhelmingly tactful from the egoic temptations he was throwing at me. How tantalizing it became as I heard how easy it would be to just say yes and to take what I had always dreamed of. But don't get it mistaken. I didn't dream of the idea of becoming a legion God for Demons. What was tempting was the power I could have within myself and the beauty I felt. The decision was easy for I knew that becoming a Demon Goddess with legions of demons would mean that others I cared for would soon fear me -which is not what I wanted...

Me:
"...No. I don't want people to fear me, and what you're offering is a lie to control me. I respectfully must deny your truce..."

Adolf Hitler:
"Fine! Then we will give you something else that could change your mind!"

In a singular motion of rage, Hitler yanked me out of the vision. Like a flash I was back on the floor with my legs and body weight still immensely heavy as can be. Unable to move from the indescribable gravity while Hunter remained in the grips of Adolf's henchmen. Furious by my rejection of the deceptive offer and with his ego bruised, with one lift of my chin saw the certainty in my eyes. He knew I wasn't going to be tempted, nor change my mind and with that, gathered dark energy into one fist and punched me unconscious.

One may be wondering…

"How can a soul become unconscious on the Astral Realms? Wouldn't you already be fully conscious the entire time?"

This is something I was confused by too. However, over the course of much heated and aggressive encounters with negatively charged spirits, I've discovered that the soul can be placed into a deep sleep even in the spirit realms and become kidnapped -which is exactly what then happened to me. With enough power (energy) from the spirit, the blow to another spirit can harm them and even make them Psychicly and consciously "checked out". These types of Psychic attacks are only done by the more powerful of entities like descended low vibrational souls like Adolf Hitler, all the way to Demons, familiar dark spirits and Devils. Energy has the power to either heal or harm and it's within the vibration of the soul that chooses what, why, and how to use their power (energy). Energy is neither good nor evil but can be altered to either form, depending on the heart (passion) of the soul.

The most I will share is that Adolf then took me to a place where I woke up on his lap in the same lingerie that I had tempted him with to rescue the girl. What he and his men did to me were things I'm not proud of and would rather leave that chapter to a close. He tortured me sexually and made me do things I wasn't aware that I was doing 'till after it was over. What Adolf was able to do was put me into a deep trance and I had forgotten who I was, and why and how I got there. It was one of the most lucid experiences I've ever had and one I will surely never forget.

Thankfully Hunter appeared and rescued me from the hell I was in and I will forever be grateful to him for that. There were also many other souls that saved me from the astral kidnapping, including my Twin Flame.

What must be noted is I was still very new to all of the astral experiences and wasn't aware of exactly what Adolf was talking about, nor did I know how to defend myself. I was still thinking small, thinking like I was only a human and fragile. But that's what spirits like Hitler want you to believe about yourself in order to continue their dark work.

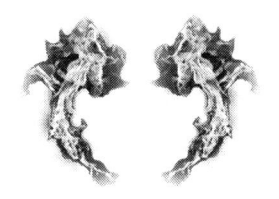

*I CAN SAY WITH ABSOLUTE CONFIDENCE, THAT AFTER MUCH MEDITATION, HEALING, SELF-LOVE, FURTHER SOULFUL ASCENSIONS AND EXPERIENCES IN BATTLE WITH DEMONS AND OTHER ENTITIES -LET'S JUST SAY HITLER GOT HIS **DUE** AND WILL CHALLENGE ME NO LONGER.*

THE WARRENS

After encountering Adolf, it became apparent quickly that even departed human souls were not only aware of me but wanted me to become aware of them. I was not so certain at first exactly just how aware they were, but over the years from researching about negatively charged humans and entities, I'd receive unfriendly greetings. This happens nearly every time when I hear or read of an entity that it has gotten to the point where I must Psychicly and astrally protect myself before I ever read about negatively charged entities including human departed souls. Some love the attention for it feeds their ego and when they know I'm either reading or learning about them, they want a piece of the astral pie so to speak. They feed off of the attention and crave the spike of altercation in hopes to get my energy one way or another.

Ed and Lorraine Warren are one of the most talked Paranormal Investigators in the field of Demonology and were well versed in their knowledge of unclean spirits. When I first heard about the Warrens, it wasn't until I discovered them after watching *The Conjuring* film -I was **HOOKED**. I had to read anything and everything about them, but more so, I wanted them to teach me all that they knew about demons and other spirits.

However, the more I read into their books, the more I started to sense a darkness surrounding me that I couldn't shake. I'd start having random demon attacks. At first it would start out as nightmares but then I'd be hearing bangs at 3 am, hear scratching sounds near my bed after waking up from a nightmare and hear voices in the house that weren't familiar. There'd be nights after a horrible nightmare of being chased or attacked by a demon that I'd wake up and smell rotten eggs or rotten meat in my bedroom. The energy would be so dark, so negative that I would be literally shaking scared and could barely move from my bed. It'd take everything in me to just walk to the bathroom because I could sense where the demon was in my room and I could see it in my third eye glaring with overwhelming intensity. But for the longest time I wasn't sure if this was just me spooking myself, so I'd try hard to tell myself it was just a dream, or that I shouldn't read the books at home or before sleeping.

No matter how many times I tried to rationalize it however, the paranormal activity continued and eventually that's when my Spirit Guides appeared and would rescue me from many attacks.

My focus through all of these experiences was to understand and hopefully uncover truths of the afterlife, the other side, our spiritual energy and how and why it all happens. Hoping that through my own paranormal experiences I could slowly understand and uncover ways on not only helping myself but how to help others. I knew that if I wanted to be a Psychic Medium, I'd have to learn not just the positive side of spirits but also the dark. Only then could I feel I was becoming the Psychic Medium I was born and meant to be. I knew that reading about them was a risk, but it was one I was willing to take in order to learn on how I could help others. But the task of learning was with a heavy heart, mind, body and faith in believing I could overcome what was haunting me. There'd be so many nights and even days where I'd be fearful to sleep and be awake in my own home. Only when I left the house did I feel safe enough to be alive or exist, for the energy would lift the moment I left just to be surrounded by other people in malls, stores or wherever I went to get back to earth. But no matter how many times I left, I knew that I eventually had to face it and conquer what was destroying faith within myself.

MELINDA KAY LYONS

After watching *The Conjuring* film in 2014, I immediately went to *Barnes and Noble* and purchased a book titled, *The Demonologist* by *Gerald Brittle*. His writing style, his authenticity to the Warrens spoke deep to me on such a personal level. The way he articulated quotes from Ed and Lorraine made me feel like I was sitting there in the houses with them as they spoke to and about demons. As they were interviewed and as Lorraine channeled information from her Psychic abilities, it felt like I was learning from the Gods of Demonology. Truly that's what it felt like.

One particular instance that I can clearly recall is when I was reading one of *Ed and Lorraine Warren's* books titled, *In a Dark Place* in 2019. Written with *Carmen Reed, Al Snedeker and Ray Garton*. Based on a true story of a nasty demon that feasts on perversion. About the Snedeker family that moved into a new home but were unaware that the house was once used as a funeral home. The Demon haunting the family, once had a powerful influence on the previous owner that triggered him to conduct necrophilia. Necrophilia is sexual interaction with a corpse, which is the kind of sexual gratification the demon craved.

Just reading the book brought back many uncomfortable memories of my own life that led to daunting triggers. There were many times I wouldn't read it again for months at a time because it was so dark.

When I reached the part where it describes how the entity appeared to Lorraine during her walk-through, that's when **SHIT**

GOT REAL. Somehow, I was suddenly there with her and could see exactly what she had experienced down in the basement. Face to face with the necrophilia perversion staring back at her. Nearly interrupted by the grossly aggravated bulge ripping the seams of his pant leg that was overshadowed by an overfed belly. It was in bad shape. The demon's entirety indulged in thirst for pain through immoral sexual demonstrations that would make the most experienced priest blush in humiliation. The entity could easily see Lorraine as she too could see it. Though the demon intended to manifest humanistic, it wasn't even close. This was a falsehood apparition from continual use of practice through centuries of human haunting.

Even though I was reading the book and could learn all of the details, I somehow was there in that moment on the Astral Realm and was experiencing all of what Lorraine had endured. Standing there looking at this entity gave me the most uncomfortable chill down my spine. Terror isn't enough to describe how frightening the presence of this spirit was. Thankfully I wasn't alone. I had Ed Warren's soul with me at the time and he was showing me what Lorraine went through. Little did I know that he would actually be there to make sure I was safe during this experience. My Spirit Guides made it aware to him that I was reading the book, but I didn't know that just by reading the true story on the Snedeker family would arouse the same demon's interest in me.

Glad isn't enough to state how happy I was that Ed was watching over me. After reading that portion of Lorraine's encounter with the demon, that same demon appeared to me that very night. I had just gone to sleep but the moment I did, I was immediately pulled out of my body and placed on the Astral Realm and there standing in front of my bed was the same corrupted perversion staring back at me. An aroma of rotten meat permeated throughout the room as it continued to stare at me in utter silence, but soon enough it spoke…

NECROPHILIA DEMON:
"…DO YOU LIKE IT WHEN I WATCH YOU UNDRESS? I'VE SEEN MANY WOMEN IN MY DAY BUT YOU'RE SOMETHIN' SPECIAL…"

While speaking in telepathy, the demon began stroking his nether lower vibrational region and it was more than disturbing to say the least. The sounds of his movements echoed like a distasteful torture in my ears.

Most Psychic Mediums and Demonologists may confuse the demon as an Incubus, but it was different. It was more like a cross between a normal demon and an Incubus. It craved the sexual perversion of children, women and found gratification through painful penetration. I know this not just from reading about it, but from countless rape nightmares that would leave me physically wounded. Each nightmare would cause me actual physical pain within my body. What was more disturbing is it would inflict it's own unclean sexual thoughts in my mind and attempt to persuade me with sex whenever I read the book. It was obvious the second I saw it, that it enjoyed my uncomfortable hardship.

The fear of the entity now mindfully undressing me made me feel all kinds of dirty that I hadn't felt with any other type of demon before. It's pulsating red veins in his eyes and neck wielded an insatiable inhumane lust for pleasure. This was one powerful son of a bitch. I ain't guna lie -I was **FUCKING SCARED**. Each looming second felt like forever. It would just stand there stroking itself as it motioned it's way toward me. Climbing it's grungy posture onto my mattress slowly pulling down my covers. Though I tried to yell at it to leave, it kept moving forward with every stroke as it continued to speak with a vile tongue.

Before I could respond a second time, Ed's soul had appeared from a light source and I could finally breathe in some ease. Without hesitation, Ed engaged the demon and told it under no certain terms that it was time to leave or that he'd make it leave. And it was in this moment Ed called for Archangel Michael and without delay the demon forcefully was pulled out of my room and taken through a portal to another dimension.

I still remember how frightful I was and continued to thank both Ed and Archangel Michael for coming to my rescue.

Though Ed is a busy soul and has much to do, he's made it his soul purpose as well as Lorraine's to watch over others from Devilish foes. I've been graced by both Ed and Lorraine's souls several times in my work on the Astral Realm and can speak wholeheartedly they're a rarity that demonology needs more of!

ANTON LAVEY: THE SATANIC BIBLE

Before you jump to conclusions -I'm **NOT** a Satanist nor do I worship Satan, the Satanic beliefs or The Satanic Bible. I read the book in 2018 in hopes to learn about **ANTON LAVEY'S** beliefs and concepts about Demons and Devils. I wanted to be able to have more of an understanding of exactly what his motives were and how he wrote the book.

Anton Szandor LaVey was an American author, musician and occultist. He was the founder of the Church of Satan and the religion LaVeyan Satanism. He authored several books, including *The Satanic Bible*.

The other reason I read it is because I get loads of specific book and film requests from fans on my YouTube channel asking me to review certain subjects or people. I take my work for helping others very seriously and will even go to the lengths of reading dark topics in order to hopefully save another person from looking into it themselves and warn them of what will happen if they do. One of the most requested topics and people for me to review was *Anton LaVey* and *The Satanic Bible*.

The Satanic Bible does have many aspects to the reality of the energy and of the other side that is factual. I can't deny this truth. Even Anton LaVey has written spiritualisms that not only validated much of what I've already come to understand and has awakened myself to accepting but it was okay to agree with even his agency of understanding. However, what he proclaims about Satanism in his definition isn't at all what it seems.

Anton mentions that the belief of Satanism is to rebel against the dogma of Christian religion and spiritual views to reclaim one's Godhood. I do highly agree on this. But that is the **ONLY** thing I am in alliance with.

What I'm against is his motives and chosen ritualist suggestive ceremonies that are low vibrational. They're surrounded by sex, dark magical rituals and are supportive to the worshipping of Satan and Lucifer as an actual entity. I can't and won't tell anyone that LaVey's ideas are positive by energetic nature, for the secret to his power I've discovered is with his allegiance with demons. Though his book describes Satan as a metaphorical example of Christian rebellion, the further one reads the easier it is to see he's merely using this to shade his darker motivations and agendas. It doesn't take a genius or a Psychic to see right through it.

Admittedly I was entranced when reading about his thoughts regardless of many disagreements. It intrigued me so much that I barely could put the book down without thinking about it afterward for hours. The most interesting aspect to the book was realizing I wasn't the only person who saw our God particle as he did and still does. Unfortunately, I also learned that he has an enlarged ego fed from his over stretched pride.

Soon enough Anton was made aware of my reading his Bible and paid me a regrettable visit. I didn't invite him, nor did I wish to talk to him. He just suddenly appeared in the middle of my bedroom one afternoon when I was reading. He articulated himself very maturely and with much knowledge. I was impressed to say the least. His appearance was like that of a sorcerer in nature accompanied with a hint of class. When I had questions about things, he answered them clearly and patiently with a soft smirk. We talked for about maybe an hour just having common ground for self-growth in one's energetic power. It seemed at first, he wasn't evil at all, nor did he make me feel uncomfortable. Surprisingly that's how he manifested and that was my initial impression -but it didn't last long.

Even though he left after conversating on polite terms, something still didn't feel right to me. I couldn't help but notice that he was looking over my shoulder and when I would turn around, there was no one there. This meeting with Anton was on the Astral Realm of course, but even on the other realms, spirits and especially demons are known to go invisible. Though I couldn't see anyone, I asked Anton casually, "What are you looking at?" But each time I asked he would shake his head saying, "NOTHING..." The smirk on his face answered different which made me *very* suspicious.

That same night, I found myself in an unforgettable nightmare that turned into another Astral Hell. I found myself in a black leather lingerie while surrounded by about ten demons and Anton sitting in front of me. He was on a large throne that was black with red fabric that he favored. His physique was masculine accompanied with a staff in hand that appointed his authority towards the demons in our presence. I didn't know what to say, but I knew I was in deep.

He continued to smooth his fingers over his glistening armrest as he said how beautiful I was. His agenda soon was revealed to be the same as the others. He was wanting me to go to his side of allegiance and without question I rejected his request. Pride and ego are the main stances for spirits that are power and control seekers like Anton LaVey. Neither in the mood to negotiate he decidedly had another trick up his sleeve and soon enough revealed Hunter in his possession.

Anton LaVey:
"...What should I do to him then? Would you be willing to let his blood be on your conscience...?"

Demons and low vibrational human souls will use leverage by capturing your departed loved ones and use them to their advantage. It's not only cunning but sickly powerful for the pain of another is unbearable to souls when they cross over and are engulfed in love.

The love Hunter and I had in our relationship at the time was beyond anything I ever experienced before that I was devoted to this love for more than a year. I refused to date anyone physically alive because the love with his soul was so real, lucid and healing. Most mystics will vote against this, but I can tell you that out of all of the relationships with live men I've had, the dead always make me feel more alive. The love with another soul that is energetically vibrational on my level is unlike any drug, alcohol or any other addictive source. The vibration one feels with a soul once ascended transcends one's perception of what it means to have love and to be loved and shapes one's own expectations to something less judgmental and egoic.

Hunter's love not only gave me a deeper sense of energy experiences but helped me heal after I was raped in 2017 by a man I tried to help. A friend of mine that I trusted and myself were at a bar and when we were waiting for a cab, decided to help this man to his home. When my friend and I were about to leave his house after making sure he was okay, he offered us a drink as a thank you. We politely denied his offer, but he was persistent and so we took a slight sip. And that's all it took for my friend to collapse to the floor and so did I.

Within seconds the man collected my paralyzed body, quickly yanked off my clothes and raped me for several hours. Most of the sexual abuse, thankfully I was unconscious, but for the first few minutes I was awake and remember much. In that unconscious state I was greeted by loving souls that told me what was happening and that it wasn't my fault. Later I learned that the man has been influenced by demons and negative spirits for most of his life and he has been doing this to girls for several years.

As much as it was painful to overcome, I became close to suicidal several times and nearly wanted to end it all. Hunter knew of my pain and was there to help me cry anytime I needed and would wake me up from a deep sleep and just hold me while I sobbed. His love, his tender voice and touch helped me on more levels than I can possibly justify and it's a gift I will forever be eternally grateful for.

So, when I saw Hunter in this moment…chained and about to be tortured by demons and Anton, I knew what had to be done. I couldn't let the one soul who was there for me get hurt. The one soul who had gave me another chance at self-love and the gift in desire to live again be ruined because of me and of my purpose. So, I gave Anton what he wanted, I gave him me.

Hunter begged me not to, but I knew that I'd not live with myself if he got harmed because of me. The torture was what one would expect, Anton had his slice of merciless greed. What made the experience more emotionally difficult was Anton made me completely forget who I was, and for a while, I thought I was Anton's wife in this astral experience. The ability he had to wipe all of my memory of myself, my daughters, and of Hunter generated more animosity within myself. I was angry, egotistical, aggressive and really believed that I suddenly was Anton's queen. The pride inside of me was not of my own, nor were the actions I portrayed towards Anton and the demons. The trance entrapped my soul to a place where I liked having sexual relations with Anton, with demons and having the power to control and hurt others. This wasn't something I was at all prepared for, nor did I ask for this to ever occur.

What most folks forget to realize, is just because I am one of the few that can fully recall this -doesn't mean it only happens to me. This type of astral attack from souls like Anton and demons can happen and does happen **ROUTINELY TO HUMANS ALL OVER THE WORLD.** The problem is most humans don't even know that it's happening because their third eye isn't opened, and their psychic abilities aren't nearly as acute.

Far few Psychic Mediums that are genuine know of this truth all too well, but the other common factor is most are fearful to come out and share their astral experiences.

My purpose in this book and with my YouTube channel was to give people a voice and to speak out about these types of hauntings. Paranormal activity is far deeper than a door opening by itself, it's a literal spiritual warfare that can lead even the strongest of hearts to kill those they love, including themselves. What Demons and familiar evil spirits are capable of is far more extensive than even the most experienced Demonologist is aware of. And that's why it's crucial that books like this are to be written to share the rawness of just how vial and diabolical it can go.

FILMS

The same happens to me whenever I watch documentaries, or films that are based on a true story. Not only has it alarmed my senses from these experiences to be more careful, but as allowed me a greater awareness in reading spirits in what they're capable of. Just by watching a movie about a demon that has been historically documented from someone else's haunting experience, can put me in astral and physical danger.

Melinda Kay Lyons

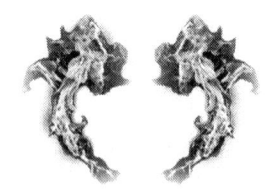

ASTRAL DANGER IS VIRTUALLY IMPORTANT. WHAT HAPPENS TO THE ASTRAL BODY IMPACTS THE PHYSICAL BODY. A HEALING ASTRAL EXPERIENCE CAN HEAL THE BODY. LIKEWISE, AN ASTRAL ATTACK TO THE ASTRAL BODY CAN EQUALLY AND NEGATIVELY IMPACT THE HUMAN BODY.

A lot of the time now since learning of this, I've been actively avoiding topics about people that are negative by nature through films and T.V. shows. It's been a rule that has served me well for the most part. But there's always those unexpected moments in film entertainment that has landed me in some of the most dangerous situations of all time. Not that I blame the documentary makers or the creators in the film business. In fact, I support their work because they help enlighten humanity on uncomfortable truths of just how dark humans can go when influenced by the wrong type of outside involvements. However, the danger doesn't step aside no matter how much I try to avoid it.

DEMON DEALER

TED BUNDY

I wish this wasn't true, boy do I wish this encounter wasn't true - but it is, nonetheless. **TED BUNDY** committed some of the most awful things to many innocent victims and has indeed created a name in history for himself. But nothing good!

Ted Bundy was an American serial killer who kidnapped, raped and murdered many young women and girls during the 1970'S and possibly earlier than that. After more than a decade of his denials, right before his execution in 1989 he confessed to 30 murders that he committed in seven different states between 1974 and 1978. This man knew how to manipulate and use people and knew how to fool people **WELL**. Very well. He was well educated and even had a family of his own at the same time while was out murdering innocent people.

There's no doubt this man was nothing short of a cold-blooded killer with nothing in his heart. His motivations for human cruelty was indescribable, and unforgettable. What brought him into my life of experiences was sorely unexpected. It was during the time I was visiting my immediate family in North Carolina in 2019. I had just arrived not a few weeks of my stay with my mother, older twin brothers and my identical twin sister before things started to go grim.

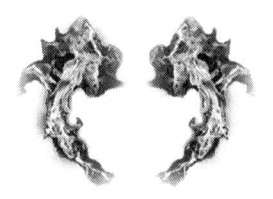

> "Doesn't working as a Demonologist put your daughter in danger? Don't you care about your daughter?"

ANGELS ALWAYS WATCH OVER MY DAUGHTER. I'VE BEEN REST ASSURED BY MY SPIRIT GUIDES AND BY ANGELS THEY ALWAYS WATCH OVER JOSSLYN ROUTINELY AND FREQUENTLY. ANGELS REQUESTED MY WORK TO CONTINUE ON EARTH AND IN EXCHANGE THEY GUARD MY DAUGHTER AS IF SHE WERE THEIR OWN.

Soon enough I was informed by my twin sister Carolyn that she was having nightmares of murder, rape and of this one man that keeps showing up in her dreams. As I listened to her story, I started to receive unnerving information in my mind's eye that seemed all too familiar. I wasn't entirely sure what spirit was causing her nightmares but then I heard and saw the word, "documentary" in my head. I then asked her,

ME:
"Have you been watching any documentaries that are about murderers by chance?"

Without missing a beat, she said…

CAROLYN:
"Oh my gosh! I've been watching documentaries about serial killers a lot lately. The one I just watched a few nights ago was about Ted Bundy."

It was then it all became clear and I suddenly remembered a dream the night before where I was standing outside my family's home and a man with glasses on approached me. He was tall, slim and wittingly attractive. But there was an aura about him that gave me an unsure vibe, but I didn't want to be rude, so I continued to talk to him. In seconds of talking with this stranger, my Twin Flame gently guided me away from him and said…

TWIN FLAME:
"Melinda, do you know who you're talking to…?"

Not sure who he was talking about, I answered…

ME:
"No…? Why? Who is he?"

Then to my utter shock he said it was Ted Bundy. Being a Psychic Medium doesn't mean you're immediately a knower of all things. Psychic abilities are much like a cosmic mind muscle that must be used and practiced in order to master and it's not always so easy to determine souls right off the bat due to their masterful disguises. Even Ted Bundy nearly fooled me into being lured away with him simply because I didn't know what he looked like. Though I've heard of him and his awful crimes, I didn't remember what his face looked like when alive.

When I shared this dream with my sister, she nearly fell off her seat in shock because she had told me she once saw a man with the same type of energy and glasses in her bedroom not too long after she watched the documentary. Thankfully she was given the instruction by my guides to stop watching those documentaries and to cleanse herself with positive thoughts and other personable instructions. I was informed that she would be closely watched over by my Spirit Guides to make sure that he wouldn't and couldn't return.

The heartbreaking part about this experience was I've met one of the women Ted had murdered. She has healed much from the hell she endured but the memory will never fully fade, and her healing process will forever be an ongoing battle. To her advantage she is given much gentle guidance, protection and love from other souls that have helped her and many of the victims along their journey. I've not met the others, but I will never forget her. Truthfully, she told me her name, but me being terrible at names I actually can't remember. I'm sure she will tell me again someday but one thing I do know is she has changed much and has even given herself a new identity, so she won't be pictured as "one of the victims of Ted Bundy". Which I fully understand and don't blame her.

As eerie as this experience was, it taught me a lot of just how powerful serial killer spirits can be. It was a teachable moment for Carolyn and I. To remember that souls of adverse intent will influence one's thoughts to be drawn to harmful and immoral subjects, people -or even in her case, documentaries. Noting it wasn't her fault but now that she's been made aware it's been a better sleeping experience for her since.

MELINDA KAY LYONS

…In order to continue **BASED ON A TRUE STORY**, I felt it was necessary and appropriate to continue this portion to, **DEVILISH ENCOUNTERS**.

EACH ENTITY DESCRIBED ARE NOT ONLY REAL BUT ARE FULLY AWARE OF YOU READING THE BOOK AT THIS VERY MOMENT. NONE ARE WITHOUT CLOSE OBSERVATION WHEN RESEARCHING THE REALM OF DEMONS, FAMILIAR DARK SPIRITS AND DEVIL ENTITIES.

TO BE CONTINUED...

DEMON DEALER

PROCEED WITH CAUTION!

Melinda Kay Lyons

DEVILISH ENCOUNTERS

CEMETERY OF THE BULL

Being a Psychic Medium I'm very well aware in the energy shifts that occur around me, including if a new spirit has entered the area that I'm in. When an Angel or another positively vibrational spirit enters the space, it will feel very lively, optimistic, loving and secure. -In fact, just today I was at a kid's Birthday party for one of Josslyn's friends and there were Angels among us. The energy was so peaceful and cheerful. I could see the Angels enjoying the party as they observed in constant gratitude. It's moments like this that remind me of how lucky I truly am in being able to see what others can't.

Although there's the obvious blessing, there's the soul crushing curse that comes with it. When a Demon or another type of negatively charged entity appears, the feeling is the exact opposite. It will feel like all hope is lost and happiness, joy and love completely abandoned my spirit. I will feel suddenly panic stricken with anxiety while dreading the idea of being alone or being in the same room with the entity that I sensed has entered the location. This feeling can be so daunting, but I've learned to face evil no matter how horrifying it may be in order to overcome this level of fear.

I can't tell you how many times I've gone to sleep and suddenly found myself in frightening situations. Nightmares by Demons and negatively charged spirits are one of the more tactful Psychic attacks and one of the most damaging to humans. Demons have insatiable abilities when given the rank of command over legions. Morbidly crossing the barriers of what is immoral, degrading and increasingly treacherous. Most humans will never know that level of hell that which must remain grateful for within the depths of the lurking doom, one will only find pain and suffering as one is chaperoned by the grace of hell's grip.

I never expected nor wanted to bare the scar of knowledge that follows down the rabbit hole that rapidly evolved into fright's basement. However, writing books that are meant to expose truth of the otherworldly brutality comes at a great cost. A payment in one's own humiliation detained by the very Demons one willingly so much as slightly mentions by name.

Each book I write about Demons isn't meant to harm or scare people, but to encourage the human race to face fear in the eye. Writing this book meant I'd have to eventually meet the Demons personally -which is **NOT** my favorite part. Each experience with an entity is unique and is regrettably hard to forget. I knew that writing this book meant I'd have to **DEAL** with limitless consequences from the passion of exposing the malice of the other side.

In summer 2019 I began to start writing about Demons for the purpose of further enlightenment but apparently one Demon had found out. The instance I began writing I had already felt something very dark in the room. No matter how many times I had tried to shake this feeling, it wouldn't fade. That same night when I attempted to sleep, I knew almost instantly something really evil was still focused on me. I didn't know what it was, but my Psychic senses picked up on how powerful it may have been, and I felt nothing but absolute fear. Knowing I couldn't do anything about it, I at least took a moment to pray for help from Angels or my spirit guides in case something were to occur. Then summed up the courage, climbed into bed and laid down to sleep.

The moment I fell asleep nearly immediately, my soul was pulled out of my body onto the astral realm and was being dragged to the ceiling by an invisible force. First it slammed me against the astral walls then to the roof. I tried to stop it, but it was too strong. It just kept tossing me around like a rag doll and when I'd try to grab it, it would hit me harder against the walls. Then in one angered motion the invisible entity punched me unconscious and that was when I woke up somewhere dark.

I remember opening my eyes to find myself in a dark place and the longer I analyzed my surroundings the more I realized I noticed rock and grass and then brought my gaze to tomb stones. I was in a cemetery. It was cold, misty and couldn't hear a sound except the sound of my fear as I breathed in trying to collect my thoughts. Breathing in and out, thinking...thinking, only to then notice there was another being behind me also breathing heavily. Before I could look at it, aggressively, it shoved my body against a large tomb stone and pinned me between the tomb and it's fowl smelling coarse hair. Unable to move an inch from the mountain of strength, the entity slammed my face into the aged stone and that was when I could see hoofs positioned by my feet. The entity was **INHUMAN**. Trembling from the cold escaping my breath while triggered with unwavering fear, hesitantly I turned to see the entity behind me.

MORAX is his name, and is one of the many with legions in his command. Thirty legions of Demons bow down at his every will and is known as the President of Hell. Some may suggest he is one to be trusted with astronomy, and all other liberal sciences -but this is **FAR** from the truth. He towers in stature, brute force and harms anyone without mercy. Appearing nearly nine feet tall, pairing a set of horns at the top of his monstrous bull skull. Each time he huffed, puffs of smoke escaped his large nostrils that sat in the sent of demonic command. Just the sight of him made me feel exceedingly small. Each time he took a step it made the ground below us quake as a hoof trampled the murky grass. I can still remember the particular sound of his hoofs and the quivery response to the shaking of his nostrils.

How the hell am I going to get out of this??!

Was the thought that surged my mind as I was restrained by one of the best of the worst kind. His dismal voice spoke in a frequency that could only leave one without hope. The very vibration to his voice made me cringe…

MORAX:
"SO, YOU WANT TO WRITE ABOUT US? DO YOU KNOW WHO I AM?"

Me:

"Yes, I want to warn people to help them. No, I don't know who you are. But you feel very respectable in your rank."

Morax:
"Very good. I am Morax, and I am considered a President of Hell."

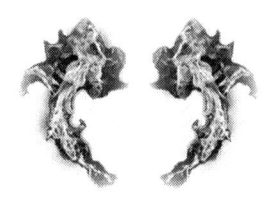

Hell and Heaven exist and don't exist. No soul is ever damned to Hell but can be taken there by Demons, Devils and other evil forces. Realms can be created by a singular consciousness or by a collective consciousness of multiple spirits from positive thoughts or negative thoughts/ frequency.

ME:
"How does one become a President of Hell? Were you elected?" (I seriously didn't know! Laugh all you want, but it was a serious question.)

MORAX:
"YOU HUMANS KNOW NOTHING OF OUR KIND... I WAS CHOSEN BY MY LORD SATAN FOR MY WORK AND OBEDIENCE TO HIM. I AM IN COMMAND OF THIRTY LEGIONS AND HAVE POWER OVER MANY."

ME:
"Is that why you're here? To show me who you are...? Do you wish for me to write about you?"

MORAX:
"YES. I'M HERE FOR YOUR KIND TO KNOW THAT I EXIST AND TO KNOW WE ARE NOT THE SUBTLE TYPE. WE DON'T TAKE WELL TO VILE TALK OF OUR KIND AND YOU'D DO WELL TO STICK TO YOUR PLACE."

I knew that him appearing in this dream was a threat of my writing ill of him, but I knew that I didn't have a choice but to stand my ground regardless of his threats... even if that meant getting hurt in the process. Obviously, I was caught off guard and without any ability at the time to get out of this situation and I felt talking to him respectfully was my only chance at getting out safely, but this duke had a temper and a **BIG** one...

ME:
"With all due respect, Morax... my place is what I am doing now, which is enlightening people and if you think your threats are going to change my mind -you're wrong."

Without much patience left in him, he grabbed my neck and squeezed tightly while bringing his face to mine. The smell from his dirty hair that coated his entire body was revolting. I could barely stand it without tears flooding my eyes, not to mention the amount of painful pressure that was closing in on my airway. Still clenching my throat, my feet left the floor as he was staring into my eyes without mercy and that's when he opened his jaw, exposing his long sharp teeth and retorted...

MORAX:
"NO? -LET ME CHANGE YOUR MIND THEN!!"

With an aggressive twist I was facing the tombstone once more and received more blows to the head. The bull beast tore my clothes off my body, pulled out chunks of my hair from yanking it violently and proceeded to rape me. The painful thrusts of the duke of hell slowly and painfully felt as if my insides were being mutilated. I could feel the inhuman shaft destroy and shatter my rib cage as the ravaging continued. All I could do was scream in agony praying it would stop at any moment. But it kept going and going and all I could summon inside was the will to survive as long as possible -but even a few seconds was far too incomprehensible.

Though the rape lasted maybe a few minutes (not sure how long it was), my Spirit Guides, and Archangel Michael appeared and saved me from the dukes uterus rampage. The dream experience felt like hours long and after they helped me heal on the astral realm, eventually I awoke from the nightmare.

When I had woken up from sleep, the nightmare wasn't caught by my memory just yet. Most often when I have nightmares or dream visits by spirits it can take several minutes, hours to even days before I fully recollect the experience. And though I didn't remember the dream yet, I do clearly recall waking up and screaming in absolute pain while clutching my stomach in the fetal position in bed. The pain was one of the worst experiences from a Demon I've ever had. I could barely walk, and when I would stand up, I couldn't help but cry as I continued to clutch my abdomen while hunched over as I very slowly walked around the house.

What led further reason of worry was when I began bleeding, but my period wasn't meant to start for another two weeks. I know my body, and it's not typical for it to start that early unless I've taken certain medications or becoming more physically active. I wasn't sexually active at this time either, so I knew there was no explanation to this. The bleeding lasted nearly a day and then it stopped and looked different from what my typical cycle would appear.

As gross and as graphic as this is, it's especially crucial to talk openly about the aftermath of Demon attacks. Men as well as women can become vulnerable in the same scenario and can be harmed in the same way. Women are not the only people Demons rape and will do so without any level of compassion accompanied.

CONSCIOUSNESS ASCENSION

Ever since that experience, I've made it a personal note to myself to expand my abilities further to the level most Psychic Mediums may not reach. This level is specifically targeted towards ones soul ascension that has become tired of restricted ways of thinking habits. When a soul ascends it will be based on their level of willingness with sheer absolute desire to expand their soul vibration to a more powerful entity. This isn't about receiving magic from an outside source. Instead, power that has always been inside one's being and is only seeking to be explored, shared, harmonized, and fully expressed without limitations.

Not to discredit nor to disrespect any other Psychic Medium or Lightworker or even to those that are awakened -however it's to be noted that most Sensitives struggle to reach this ascension point due to restrictive ideals, fear, doubt and even religious views that prevent them from ascension.

Souls are not meant to be commanded by a God entity.

WE ARE GOD ENTITIES AND ARE FULLY CAPABLE OF BANISHING DEMONS, DEVILS AND ANY OTHERWORLDLY DARK FORCES.

I speak of one's God particle as discussed prior. Harnessing this particle allows the soul to continue to expand at such an exceptionally fast speed as long as the mind of the soul is willing to let go of fear, doubt, insecurities and remain focused on the overall goal in one's purpose. Love accompanied with this in mind, gives the Lightworker, Psychic Medium and even Demonologist a distinct advantage -and that's exactly what

DEMONS DON'T WANT YOU TO KNOW!!

Once I made the decision to expand my horizons and was tired of being defenseless, I began learning with my spirit guides and through my abilities on how to fight demons. The only way one is able to get to this level is their consciousness must first go through a stage of pain to then be fully ready to expand their conscious awareness. This isn't just a choice, on the contrary. It's a soulful energetic shift that occurs within one's vibration that begins to evolve past ego, past one's own perception and releases one's fears.

Granted, there will be some ascensions that will be bestowed to one's soul by other advanced entities, such as

ASCENDED MASTERS or
LORDS OF THE UNIVERSE.

Then there's the other ascensions where the soul suddenly shifts to different levels of conscious awareness and perspective in sight, sound, feelings, thoughts, choices, intentions, etc. Not all people will experience the same type of ascension processes, but they happen frequently as long as the soul either living or departed is consistently working on bettering themselves and learning the art of self-mastery on an energetic and emotional level.

One Demonic torture in particular that was the worst type of hell I'm still haunted by that I can't even mention it in this book -even that experience most definitely triggered my soul to finally escape from mindful limitations. Because of this, I've ascended several times and am now considered an exceptional level.

Not sure I will fully reveal to the general public what my ascension level is for I don't want you or others to get the wrong idea of my intentions. I'm not one to boast, nor do I intend to have people suddenly fearing or worshipping me -that's literally insane. Though I'm a highly spiritual woman, I'm still realistic with common sense and wouldn't want you to suddenly start making shrines with my name. That's just creepy. No... what I prefer is for you to know my experience as an ordinary person that's simply learned from her hell and how she found her own heaven. In hopes that in sharing my story will empower your own.

My experiences have driven me to expand so fast that I'm no longer as fearful of Demons like I once was. Don't get me wrong, I am still fearful of Demons, but it's changed dramatically thanks to my extensive ascended training. Training with some of the best and highly evolved souls, including Yehoshua, I've learned many ways in how to defend myself against Demons on the astral realm and how to help others. Since then, my way of **DEALING** with demons has been significantly *different.*

THE ROYAL BEDCHAMBER

If you've ever seen the film *Hereditary* that was made in 2018, I'm sure you're fully aware of this Demon king. He's exceptionally powerful, high in rank and is considered one of the most devoted Demons to Lucifer. He is most recognized in *The Goetia of King Solomon* written by *Aleister Crowley* that was first published in 1904.

KING PAIMON is considered the Ninth Demon in the Descended Hierarchy and is very obedient unto Lucifer. He is known to appear to humans in the form of a confident man that sits on a dromedary with a shiny crown upon his head. His attire is wealthy in splendor similar to an Arabian king, draped in rich red fabric, while covered in jewels following the royal taste to his chosen pleasure. King Paimon will not show another respect unless is addressed by his royal title accompanied with a bow and perhaps an offering.

Out of all of the Demons I've personally encountered, this one is a special sort that is rare to come by. Use of his very tongue will be heard with great wisdom, knowledge, teaching in all arts, sciences and a many other secrets. -But don't let his glamour fool you, for he is a malicious king in command of 200 legions of Demons and other lower vibrational beings.

Granted one can simply read information online or by purchasing a book, which is exactly what I did at first after upon watching the film *Hereditary*. I've never heard of this Demon before, so I began to research him online. However, the more I read on him the more I realized I couldn't help but want to meet him for some crazy reason. Call me nuts -but I was **HOOKED**. I couldn't stop thinking about this entity and the more I pushed him out of my head, the more I heard his name all day repeating like a broken record in my mind. There was something significant about this Descended King that literally bewitched me. I can't explain it other than that. His very name, the images, the descriptions…it was almost as if he was calling out to me, for I could see him clearly in my mind's eye as if I was meant to meet him.

What many are not aware of and what took me awhile to learn, is this repetitiveness of his name, the images in my mind, etc., is a type of demonic attack to lure you. They **WANT** you to contact them.

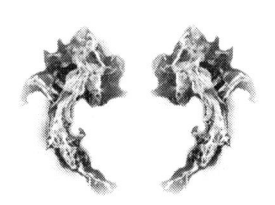

DEMONS ARE KNOWN FOR BEING MIND READERS AND MANIPULATORS OF OUR DARKEST EMOTIONS, FEARS AND DESIRES. DEMONS ARE ALSO MOST NOTORIOUS FOR IMPLANTING THEIR NAME AND IMAGE IN YOUR HEAD FOR YOU TO WANT TO CONTACT THEM. THIS IS WHAT I CALL, **PSYCHIC ENTRAPMENT.** WHERE THE DEMON REPEATS IMAGES, THOUGHTS, FEELINGS, SOUNDS INTO THE PERSON'S MIND SO AS TO TRICK THEM TO DO THINGS THEY WOULDN'T NORMALLY DO.

What I wasn't aware of at the moment or for days, was he knew I had been reading about him from curiosity after watching the film in mid 2019. Due to that curiosity, he began putting his image and name in my mind so much that I eventually decided one night in a dream state on the astral realm to summon the Ninth Descended King.

I know what you're probably thinking...

What the hell Melinda?! Are you crazy?! Are you suddenly becoming a Demon worshipper now?

Firstly, I was definitely crazy in that moment. I admit that fully. But sometimes in order to know exactly what you're dealing with, sometimes knowledge has to be summoned in order to learn it for yourself.

I would criticize *Zak Bagans* for doing this exact thing on his show *Ghost Adventures on Travel Channel* -the difference is I don't do it on camera and never will. Does this mean I will be summoning Demons to get information out of them regularly? -No and **NEVER** again! I understand now why someone like Zak would do such risky experiments, as I have been involved within the same boat of desperate curiosity, but I **NEVER** recommend it to anyone, and I'll explain why.

When I had summoned King Paimon, I conducted it on the astral realm in my bedroom where I literally created the ritual. I remember drawing out the giant circle on the floor by manifesting chalk magically in my hand, along with a number of other tools that were required simply by the snap of a finger.

This is done by the mindfulness of the soul on the other realms. All spirits dead or alive can do this once in the awareness of their own energy capabilities. With practice I've been able to manifest nearly anything to my heart's content on the astral realm. I've been able to even change my clothes, hair color and length, all the way to altering my very physical appearance. Once a soul ascends, one is capable of nearly anything you can imagine for it's a realm of limitless possibilities which is one of the leading reasons to why I'm so addicted to the other side.

Soon I manifested candles and had them lit in the right positions and even faced myself to the West of earth which is required when summoning this Demon king.

You may be wondering why I chose to summon him on the astral plane and not on the physical plane. The answer may be obvious to the experienced of this realm, but I chose the astral realm because I just HAD to see him.

The astral realm is beyond lucid in sight, taste, touch, smell, sound and emotions. It's extremely vivid and can make you so overwhelmed with just how real this realm actually is once you've learned how to get their simply by conscious choice. I knew that if I wanted to meet King Paimon, then I'd have to do it on that realm to see just how clear he may appear if he did in fact exist. I was stubborn and very naive. I refused to believe that all entities listed in books are real unless I fully experienced them personally for the first time. And I knew that if there was one Demon I would openly summon, it would be this king out of all Demons.

Once the ritual was set, I began the ceremony. May be hard to believe, but I even managed to manifest a demonology book in my hands that had exact instructions on how to properly prepare for such rituals. When I found the right book after scanning thousands in a flash in my mind, I immediately snapped my fingers and the book appeared from out of stardust. I guess you could say I really was Sabrina the teenage witch for a minute.

Once the ceremony begun, I had to chant specific words that I honestly don't remember anymore. However, once I got the hang of it, I focused with all of my energy and emotions in respect of King Paimon to summon him to appear. What felt like nearly thirty minutes of this, suddenly a large booming sound followed with very loud trumpets and music echoed in the entire space. It was so abrupt that it nearly frightened me. To my utter shock, a light began to emerge from thin air, then circulated into a portal made of flame and to appear through this portal was King Paimon riding his dromedary and two of his most loyal of Demons at his side.

All I can say is I was absolutely speechless in this moment. I didn't know what to do or what to say. But I knew I had to say something so I then attempted to stand and address him as formal as I could. But without apology, in reaction King Paimon's grungy appearance then supported an extremely loud voice that I swear could've been heard on the physical realm. This part is known in many writings as a warning of caution. When one is intending to summon King Paimon, one must then say certain phrases and words amidst the ear drum breaking experience. The voice is nothing I've ever heard before. It truly is painful, unbearable and even hurts you physically on the astral realm if not done carefully because it's THAT loud and **PAINFUL** to hear.

Struggling with all of my might to do this right, I continued repeating the phrases that are meant to be said a certain amount of times and when I met his requirements, suddenly he stopped and his whole physical appearance was just like what I had heard and read about.

His very presence on his dromedary was extraordinary. I was bewitched by how undoubtedly handsome he appeared while draped in glamour beyond earth's capabilities. There are different types of textures, minerals, fabric and even metals in the other worlds and it was truly a sight to see. I won't lie. He was something to witness indeed. I felt I was in the presence of a king and someone who would and could so easily cut off my head if I wasn't careful. -be reminded, this is a Demon lord. His very wardrobe matched his dromedary and his loyal servants along with their weapons at their sides. What got me more intrigued was how his voice suddenly became soft and sharp at the same time…

KING PAIMON:
"…YOU SUMMONED ME…?"

ME:
"…Yes, great and noble King."

KING PAIMON:
"…I SEE. … MOST MEN ARE NOT ABLE TO SURPASS MY SUPREME VOICE… BUT HERE I AM GREETED BY A SMALL GIRL THAT SEEMS TO HAVE A UNIQUE TOLERANCE THAN MOST. I AM IMPRESSED."

It's important to note, my quotes of King Paimon are nowhere close to how well he speaks. His choice in words is exceptionally clever and tactful with centuries of experiences. I'm barely scratching the surface of what I can remember as to exactly what he meant in how he spoke. I'm not great at speech by any means, and he knew this but even then, he continued as who he is.

KING PAIMON:
"...WHAT IS IT YOU REQUEST FROM ME?"

Most people view King Paimon similar to like a genie in a bottle, asking him for fame, money, love, riches -but I had something different in mind…

ME:
"King Paimon…I request nothing from you that is made by man nor by this forsaken earth that withers by our doing. What I seek is guidance, and deeper knowledge into your kind and of your lordship. I want to understand more secrets of the world, and humbly request that I may simply have a few hours to speak with you…"

I remained bowed in respect to his time in appearing willingly. I could feel his sight upon my shoulders and my lowered head, and knew he was more intrigued for then I heard him dismount his dromedary. His shoes of soft cloth barely made a sound as he walked my way slowly. Then gently lifted my head with his fingers under my chin, and that's when I could see brilliant colors dancing in his eyes. I've never seen such magic in a Demons eyes before. Again, he bewitched me…

KING PAIMON:
"YOU ARE INDEED A RARITY. THOSE THAT CALL MY NAME ONLY SEEK LOVE THEY CANNOT GET, MONEY THEY CANNOT WIN, FAME THAT ISN'T THEIRS AND YET... YOU ONLY WISH TO SPEAK WITH ME? IS THERE NOT ANYTHING YOU WISH FOR DEAR GIRL?"

ME:
"The things I desire are not of this world your highness. Though there are many tangible desires that are indeed tempting, they would never truly satisfy me. What I desire is knowledge, enlightenment, power within myself, love and a many other things that money cannot buy, and a spell cannot cast."

KING PAIMON:
"OH, I CAN MAKE ANYONE FALL IN LOVE WITH ANYONE. THAT CAN CERTAINLY BE DONE IF YOU WISH. JUST POINT HIM OUT... OR HER...IF THAT IS WHAT YOU LIKE..."

ME:
"...Certainly, I have no doubt in your ability to conjure miracles and impressive otherworldly power, but I would rather have love be of the heart, not of a spell. But thank you my lord for the offer. I am grateful."

That was when he kneeled down as I sat on the floor. At the time I didn't feel even standing was respectful to his rank, but truth be told I was also fearful of doing the wrong thing. When he kneeled at my level, I remember our eyes met and was mesmerized by the sparkles of power that seemed like an enchanted dancers game. I couldn't take my eyes off of him.

Eventually a sensually alluring scent captured my senses. He smelled like an otherworldly cologne for men that I can't explain. It was so scrumptious to the senses that I couldn't stand not being near him. When he recognized my interest heightening, he stood me up and then we sat at two royal like chairs that he manifested by a simple wave of his hand. Upon sitting, I was able to ask him questions and see what he had to say about the other side, Demons and about how they work in their hierarchy. I learned much just by talking with him. Pondering back on this memory now, I'm still very grateful for this talk with him and always will be because I truly learned a lot. This one on one experience with King Paimon is one I'll always treasure - **but only this first moment.**

The more we began to talk, the more I realized he made me feel feelings for him. It started to evolve rather quickly the more he was gently complimenting my aura, appearance and how much he could sense my energetic level. The fact he could read me so well intensified my interest alarmingly fast, though I was so involved I didn't even realize how much this interest quickened.

Our conversation led to many questions. The more he spoke the more questions I had. One in particular that I remember is asking about **S**UCCUBUS Demons. I've never personally met one before, and only had encountered **I**NCUBUS. And in that one comment, he suddenly had two of his most loyal Succubus appear before my very eyes. They were indeed beautiful, but let's be honest, in a sort of classless way. They weren't charming to say the least and were egotistical about their appearance. When I made a slight compliment on how beautiful they were even for a Demon, they had this attitude about them that said, "I know!". It wasn't humble and it wasn't attractive. Though their wings, ample breasts and even perfectly round buttock could've been shaped by the Gods, their attitudes were shady, crude and arrogant. Not to forget their eyes were blood red with a body full of spikes and supported by gargoyle feet. These female Demons were nearly seven or eight feet tall. It was amazing but disturbing to say the least. What I found disgusting was their immediate behavior. Once aware of this, I was reminded that I was in the company of Demons and had to remain on guard.

While still in conversation with one of the Kings of hell, I began to feel a bit different. My thoughts and emotions were beginning to feel a bit lost, unsure of where I was and even confused. Just looking around was making me a bit woozy, that's when what seemed like a conversation between two mature beings, ended in a situation I didn't expect.

King Paimon while staring at me adamantly, began to suggest the end of his bargain...

KING PAIMON:
"...I HAVE GIVEN YOU MY TIME IN EXCHANGE AS YOU'VE ASKED. BUT NOW IT IS TIME YOU GIVE ME SOMETHING ELSE IN EXCHANGE AS AN OFFERING - AS PAYMENT."

ME:
"You're right, forgive me. I had nearly forgotten this agreement because I've enjoyed this enlightened talk greatly. What is it most people offer you my King?"

I said while still being a bit hazy...

KING PAIMON:
"...MOST PEOPLE OFFER ME THEIR ALLEGIANCE BUT THERE ARE OTHER THINGS THAT CAN BE OFFERED. BUT THIS IS UP TO YOU AND MUST MEET THE FAIRNESS OF WHAT I HAVE BESTOWED."

His tone dramatically changed with a slight roughness to his command. For quite a time this Demon King demonstrated as a groomed and classy magician, but the more he requested for his "payment", the more his tone and facial appearance slowly altered…

ME:
"I'm not sure what to offer you for I'm sure you have all of what you've ever desired considering your position. As a Demon king, what could I offer that would quench your payment owed?"

KING PAIMON:
"…YOU ARE CORRECT AGAIN. I HAVE ALL THAT I COULD EVER DESIRE. I HAVE ALL THE RICHES, POWER AND CONTROL THAT A MAN COULD EVER DREAM OF -EVEN POSSESSION OF AS MUCH FEMALE PUSSY I COULD DEMAND."

I was instantly caught by surprise. Easily my face adjusted to the shock in my expression from the sudden sexual explicitness he so openly divulged. Again, I was reminded that he was a Demon King and was not to be trusted. However, as untrustworthy as he is and knowing this entirely, there was still some kind of sexual attraction that I couldn't articulate. The very "P" word suddenly didn't bother me, nor did I feel any type of offense from his sexual perversion. In fact, I was becoming more interested in this King…

ME:
"...Typically, I hate that word, but somehow it doesn't bother me... and I don't know why."

KING PAIMON:
"OH? - THERE'S NOTHING WRONG WITH ENJOYING THE SIMPLE PLEASURES OF ONE'S BODY AND OTHERS. SEX ISN'T SOMETHING YOU SHOULD BE ASHAMED OF, ESPECIALLY... IF IT MAKES YOU BLUSH LIKE HOW YOU ARE RIGHT NOW..."

I didn't realize I was blushing. The fact that I was, made me wonder why and even became embarrassed so much so that I couldn't look directly at him anymore. Being so entranced by his still seductive voice, I only then examined the room to realize the succubus had left without a sound. It was now only me and the Demon King, alone...

ME:
"I didn't realize we were already alone. I'm sorry, I hope I didn't overtake your time. I don't know what I can give you King Paimon, but I'd like to give you something in return, but I do not know what would satisfy you."

The King's eyes lingered from mine then slowly motioned down my body. The focus of his eyes as they examined every inch of me began a surge of energy that overtook my whole internal and mental focus. The energy felt like he was slowly undressing me with sexual satisfaction beyond my wildest dreams. His physical examination felt like a few minutes too long, but I somehow didn't care. I liked his attention and I couldn't seem to understand why I would even want it.

HE'S A DEMON KING FOR CRYING OUT LOUD!!

-But I didn't care. I wanted his focus all on me for the temptation luring inside of me seemed oh so sweet. I didn't want this moment with him to end.

King Paimon nonchalantly began smoking what looked like an otherworldly cigar as he leaned back in his chair of natural command. Sending darts of sexual persuasion through his sharp eyes while I was now experiencing an intensive hormonal flame arousing my every desire. Then swiftly within the spark of this quiet but breathless moment, I began having rapid visions of him and I together. I could feel the sense of his touch, the sensuality of his power charging my sexual battery as we mended our energetic bodies together. The visions were so undeniable that it took everything in me to try to push the thoughts out, that once again presented a rosy flush upon my face.

Amusement slid across his when I began to notice I was breathing heavily and uncontrollably. Stunned and embarrassed I quickly apologized...

ME:
"I'm sorry, I don't know what's going on but... I keep having these weird...thoughts in my head and it's not like me. I apologize."

KING PAIMON:
"...OH? WHAT THOUGHTS? I'D VERY MUCH LIKE TO KNOW..."

He said as he exposed an effortless smile that revealed nothing imperfect with a dash of shimmer from his pearly chomps...

ME:
"...These thoughts just came into my mind at random, I think. I don't know where they came from. I'm too embarrassed to say, but I won't allow it to happen again, -I'm sorry."

KING PAIMON:
"...I SEE... I HAVE EVERYTHING I'VE EVER WANTED AND COULD EVER DESIRE, BUT THE ONE THING I DON'T HAVE IS... -WELL NOW I'M SHY TO TELL YOU..."

ME:
"Wait? You get shy? I thought Demons don't have those kinds of emotions…"

KING PAIMON:
"OH YES, WE HAVE ALL KINDS OF EMOTIONS. BUT I'M NOT YOUR ORDINARY DEMON MELINDA."

He said with another intense gaze into my eyes…

ME:
"No, of course not. You're right. Forgive me. I only assumed all Demons were brutally mean. You however… you're… different. You almost don't seem like a Demon at all. You seem more… like a human."

As Paimon took one last hit from his cigar and flicked it to the floor, he then scooted his chair closer with full intention to have his legs now touching mine. His knee now grazing the edge of my skin might as well have been an invitation to jump right in. (Some how I keep rhyming). The thought of this wouldn't escape my mind. The thought of my energy mending with his, and experiencing love making with a Demon king surprisingly became my own desire. It was all I could think about…

KING PAIMON:
"…I'VE BEEN WITH MANY WOMEN THAT HAVE GIVEN ME ALL OF THE KIND OF SEXUAL ENCOUNTERS ONE COULD EVER EXPERIENCE. I'M ALREADY VERY SATISFIED"

ME:
"So… you don't desire anything more meaningful?"

KING PAIMON:
"YOU MEAN LOVE?"

ME:
"Yes…"

The King leaned back in his chair once again and shifted his head casually in an upward position so as to look down at me without interest. Playing it cool as he answered…

KING PAIMON:
"...NO. I DON'T NEED LOVE. I HAVE PLENTY OF LOVE OF MY SERVANTS AND GET WHATEVER IT IS THAT I COULD EVER WANT. I DON'T NEED LOVE TO FULFILL ME. I HAVE ALL THAT I NEED."

ME:
"I see. But love is something so much deeper and more powerful. You can have sex with as many women as you so choose but without love it is all meaningless and leads to nothing but a hollow heart."

KING PAIMON:
"IF I DIDN'T KNOW ANY BETTER, I'D GUESS YOU'RE A NATURAL POET. INTERESTING... TELL ME MORE ABOUT THIS LOVE THAT YOU BELIEVE I NEED."

ME:
"...Well... love is an energetic formula to the soul that enables one to a higher level of vibration that surrenders to pure energy. Not surrendering to helplessness, but to what is all good and generous. (There I go, rhyming again). Love shared by two souls generates healing and a spark of electric transformation that gives both souls the ability to grow together. It's like one's life jacket to healing, that saves one from drowning in sorrow and misery. I am shy when it comes to

sex on a certain degree, but when it is followed by love it can be a very transformative experience that blossoms oneself similar like a flower in spring."

King Paimon:
"Interesting... so are you saying that I need love?"

Me:
"I'm not sure my King. But if you've not ever experienced love before, then perhaps -but that's not for me to decide."

King Paimon gave another smirk as he ever so smoothly brushed his leg against mine. With a smooth reach from behind me he placed his fingers in my hair and began massaging the back of my neck.

I knew this was a Demon. I knew he wasn't to be trusted, but I couldn't ignore how stimulating his touch was on my skin. The pressure of his fingertips from this massage brought a sudden heatwave throughout my body. Not chills, but **HEAT**. A rush of unexplained warmth ran through me like I was suddenly in a hot furnace of the Devil's house. I couldn't waiver from the prolonging urge that I so desperately wanted to explore. The sexual desire was beyond overwhelming and he knew it…

KING PAIMON:
"I CAN GIVE YOU SOMETHING THAT LOVE CAN'T... SOMETHING THAT WOULD MAKE YOUR LEGS QUIVER..."

ME:
"Nothing against you, but I've had more than my fair share of love making that's made me plenty satisfied."

KING PAIMON:
"NOT LIKE THIS YOU HAVEN'T... HAVEN'T YOU WANTED TO EXPERIENCE WHAT I CAN DO TO YOUR BODY?... WHAT YOU KNOW YOU CAN'T GET FROM ANYONE ELSE?... COME ON MELINDA, I KNOW YOU THOUGHT ABOUT IT... THOUGHT OF WHAT I COULD DO TO YOU..."

The more he spoke the more it greatly enhanced the powerful urge of sexual desire. His voice inside my ear made my senses relax and tense up at the same time. The more he tempted me, the greater it all became more tantalizing to my bodice. I wanted him to touch me, I wanted his voice inside of me to keep talking... I wanted him **ALL THE WAY**.

The next few things he said in my ear were derogatory and degrading but it just stimulated my sense to what felt like the strongest sexual desire I've ever encountered. My eyes were closed as he continued to whisper succulent sexual temptations in my ear and the next thing I knew, I suddenly did the unthinkable…

ME:
"-I'll give you me."

KING PAIMON:
"-ARE YOU SURE? IS THAT WHAT YOU AGREE IN EXCHANGE FOR PAYMENT??"

ME:
"Yes…"

And that was it. I was out like a light and suddenly woke up somewhere else. Where I was, was unlike anything I've ever experienced before. Granted I've had the undoubted blessing and gift to experience plenty of beautiful moments and sights with positive spirits, Angels and other entities -but this was *significantly* different.

I found myself somewhere unique to the eye's pleasure, for each place where I laid my sight upon, was nothing short of gratifying. I found myself in a room where I was laying on a bed, and a massive bed at that. As I sat up unsure where I was or how I got here, I took time to examine the room but to my surprise seemed I was in an exotic dream. I was sure of it.

This place was beautifully decorated with expensive fabrics, pleasing smells, sex appeal, glamour, gold and gems. I swear it felt like I was suddenly in an Arabian palace that could only be summoned or created by the most holy and prestige. Placed in the King's royal bedchamber waiting for his highness's arrival to come and sweep me off my feet. And swept I most certainly was! The overall scenery of this space would easily convince even masters of illusion as each inch was entailed in majestic splendor. As I was taking in the lavishness of my surroundings and walking around, I came to find a mirror and became speechless to what I had discovered.

Upon seeing within the mirror that was framed in gold and jewels was me dressed in the finest and softest red silk-like fabric supported by a golden fragile belt along my waist. Graciously astounded by the slightest push of my bosom in what appeared to be supported by a golden breast plate that was engraved in diamonds, crystals and other assorted gems. Too mesmerized by the sight of brilliant shimmer as if one hundred million stars were the culprit to my now muted amazement. Only for my eyes to catch the glimpse of thick wavy long hair that I could never grow with a glistening golden crown that lay poised atop my effortless styled locks...

How could this be?! How beautiful?! Is this all a dream??

I continued to ask myself as I couldn't stop but maintain absolute undivided attention on the glory of my body figure that had indeed changed. Being human with my own insecurities, I was certain this was most definitely a dream, but even so I didn't want to awake for the wonder was too magnetic to escape. The spell of sheer beauty overtook my every deepest desire that my eyes began to swell in tears. Being draped in the finest upon finest of what my ordinary mind could imagine had been amplified beyond measure. The scars on my face from years of severe acne, and lines of age had all but vanished. My heart's strings were pulled open as if all of my longing of wandering imagination could take me had drifted my soul into what could only be identified as utter fantasy.

As my tears fell from overwhelming gratitude, it was then I saw King Paimon arrive from a portal-like doorway. His attitude was the same as before, only more interactive socially. When he entered the room, I instantly knew who he was and without hesitation pointed my way towards him and bowed in obedience and respect. The Demon King smoothly lifted my chin up towards him with one hand, and replied…

KING PAIMON:
"A QUEEN…DOES NOT BOW TO HER KING…"

He said while carrying a smirk on his perked lip of satisfaction. Paimon much rather enjoyed my envy and respect during this exotic entrapment.

Full of boast and oversized ego, he carried conversation on about himself of the many palaces he claims to have all over the world and universe. I sat and listened to his lick of talk about his ability in power and command of over 200 legions that fear and honor him. He was charming in this moment. I can't lie, I truly was mesmerized. The time we spent here in this dreamlike fantasy, enchanted me with diamonds, gold, beauty, rank and power. Needless to say, I felt like I had found another godlike entity I could learn from and possibly emulate to a slight degree with more charm. Even for a Demon lord, he complimented on my abilities and energetic ascension. To be so graced with his approval meant everything to me. I was in a daze full of envy over his presence alone. My eyes danced like a fire blaze as he would teach me things of the universe and the world. I learned much from him about demons, the power and command he upheld and passion for what he wanted. I had believed and supported it all.

It was like a dreamer's dream come to life, but it didn't cost him much time to suggest that I give myself to him as agreed. And in that, King Paimon and I entered his bed draped in miles of gold and a blood silk…

BEFORE YOU FREAK OUT…KEEP READING…

As romantic as this may have sounded of King Paimon and my intimacy, what at first was a sensual partnership began to demonstrate degrading and painful intercourse. He quickly began to get violent, aggressive, and wanted me do things that I said no to. When he couldn't get me to do everything he demanded, it greatly angered him. His voice changed to something dark and unsettling and then he quickly motioned himself to me. Slowly soft fingers caressed my cheek and told me to look deep into his eyes. At first, I was reluctant from the pain I had felt, but here he felt safe once more, and it was here that I suddenly flew into his eyes and was somewhere else.

In a flash I was somewhere out in the middle of a desert and unable to get back. I then heard his voice echo loud with laughter as he said...

King Paimon:
"You do as I say or suffer from the hands of my legions. You don't want to know what they'll do to you..."

Immediately I could hear an enormous mob of Demons of all shapes and sizes echo a chant as they charged my way across the heat-stricken desert. Panicked and unable to get out, I called out to my guides and Angels but Paimon laughed a second time responding with...

KING PAIMON:
"...THEY CAN'T HEAR YOU MELINDA. YOU'RE IN MY WORLD NOW. NO ONE HERE CAN HEAR YOU SCREAM. IF YOU WANT OUT, YOU MUST REMAIN MINE AS AGREED OR SUFFER AT THE CLAWS OF MY ARMY."

I began to feel fire, pain and suffering take over me and couldn't seem to find anyway to escape. I literally felt like I was being burned alive though my skin seemed untouched. All I could do was cry with panic but knowing his army was soon to engage in my capture, I reluctantly agreed...

With another jerk of a Psychic pull, suddenly I was back in the bloodthirsty bed and was no longer myself again. I had completely forgotten who I was and wanted nothing but to please my great descended King. I can still recall the visions he implanted into my vulnerable mind of blood and pain caused around the world as he had his way. The more we were together the more I felt extremely drained and powerless. I couldn't hold myself up and felt like my whole energy source within myself had evaporated. For what I didn't realize at this time was as he and I were being sexually involved, he was stealing my soul energy and **RAPIDLY**.

When he was done, he had gotten up and dressed himself in a pair of otherworldly fabric that covered his legs and groin just enough similar to like pants that was also supported by a large golden belt full of rubies. I remember looking up at him in a state of euphoria as I craved his physique that stood before me. The soft tan and the washboard abs made me have to take more than a second look to capture the memory of his beautiful figure. Even his brown hair that touched his shoulders didn't sway my intensified attraction and he loved every minute of it.

There was motion of attention in Paimon as another entity had entered the room. It was a Demon dressed in what appeared to be like military armor of another world. It was surreal to see the light dancing off of the Demons otherworldly metals and materials that represented demonic authority. King Paimon had then been requested to speak to "him" in private. King Paimon did not delay for he knew that it was by the request of his most trusted master.

Before leaving, King Paimon approached me holding what appeared to be a beautiful necklace. He draped it around my neck as what I assumed was a gift of obedience. It's glistening chatter instantly caught my attention as he gently locked it around my neck. Once the bedazzled present was secured, King Paimon transformed into his original attire, and exited the room.

Excited to see this necklace I took a gander at myself in the once again tall golden mirror to see how it gleamed upon my neck…

Unknown Voice:
"It's pretty isn't it my queen? The King certainly has good taste, doesn't he?"

Alarmed, I jumped to my surprise as I caught a glimpse of a hunched over Demon that had been watching me in the corner for some time. Apparently, he had been there for a long while. It was then I stood in absolute confidence in the nature of slight humility and replied…

Me:
"Yes. I appreciate him greatly. …What is your name Demon?"

The Demon was just about to speak it's name but not too soon before a second appeared to also announce himself. They both stood not but a few feet tall for their very nature seem to be that of a crouched servant. Their mannerism indicated they had been long time obedient followers of King Paimon, and it wasn't long until they confirmed my hunch…

Demons:
"We are Labal and Abalim. We are kings under our King's command and are loyal servants of our master."

Hunched and crawled like animals, they eventually came in the moonlight that quickly highlighted the minion Demon kings from a nearby window. It was without question these two were Demons but nearly reminded me of something like a disfigured pet or even a human.

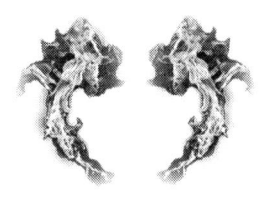

IT'S CRUCIAL TO NOTE THAT MY OWN EXPERIENCES MAY NOT ALWAYS MATCH THE EXACT DEFINITIONS OR APPEARANCES OF THE DEMONS THAT ARE LISTED PUBLICLY. DEMONS ARE KNOWN TO ALTER THEIR APPEARANCE AS OFTEN AS THEY CHOOSE REGARDLESS OF WHAT HUMANS CLAIM THEM TO BE. HOWEVER, IT'S SAFE TO SAY THAT NEARLY MOST OF MY EXPERIENCES HAVE INDEED MATCHED MUCH OF WHAT ANCIENT TEXTS HAVE IDENTIFIED THESE AND OTHER ENTITIES AS.

What felt like days, even months in this palace was merely a few hours during sleep state. And though I had forgotten all of who I was and never seemed to mind that I was engaging laughter with King Paimon's Demon kings, I then began to feel odd. As I was talking with the Demons, I then heard a voice inside my head that I didn't recognize at first…

TWIN FLAME:

"Melinda… Are you okay?? Please tell me you can hear me!"

ME:

"Yes… I can hear you. -But who is this?"

TWIN FLAME:

"Oh my god Melinda… you really don't remember who I am?"

ME:

"No sir, and you'd be wise to not address me so casually…"

TWIN FLAME:

"Oh, I'm sorry… you're right. My apologies… but how should I address you?"

ME:

"Highness will do fine."

TWIN FLAME:

"Your Highness, may I as so gracefully have the pleasure of allowing myself to speak with you…?"

ME:

"Yes, what is it you need to speak about? -But do so with haste for my King should return before sunrise."

(I'm fully aware that I sounded much like a pompous ass).

My Twin Flame knew that I was not myself and was worried on how he was going to get me to remember who I was. He took a moment to think of something, for the only way he could come and get me is if I welcomed him into the palace portal entrance. That's when he said…

TWIN FLAME:

"Melinda -I mean, your highness… I am faced with a great dilemma where myself and my friends are in great need to rescue someone I love and care about. But she does not remember who she is. What do you think I should do?"

ME:

"…Well that would depend. Is she in danger?"

TWIN FLAME:

"Yes! In **GRAVE** danger."

ME:

"I see. That is serious… Does she love him back?"

He paused for a moment and then said humbly…

TWIN FLAME:

"She did once, but I've hurt her more than she ever deserved in the past. I wish I could take everything back that I've ever done, but even I don't deserve someone as amazing and beautiful as her. I am no one special, but I love her immensely and would do anything for her to be safe and to get her back. Even if she never loved me again, which I don't blame her, I just want her safe and happy."

ME:

"I see. Pain is indeed a lesson -painful but a lesson, nonetheless. If she truly loved you before the betrayal, then eventually she shall forgive you and all will be in harmony once more because there is love between you both."

TWIN FLAME:

"Thank you, your highness, I will take your wisdom to heart as always. But can I perhaps bestow to you information of her and myself so as to maybe enlighten me further on other complications that have arrived? It's greatly complex and I feel you would be perfect to tell me what you sense…"

I generously agreed and within seconds of quieted focus on my Twin Flame, I felt his energy begin to tap into mine through the power of thought. This thought wave linked our souls together nearly effortlessly, and it was in that moment my heart source opened. My emotions bewildered me to tears but then it was also in this moment I recollected myself and realized I was in **SERIOUS SHIT!**

ME:

"-Oh my God!! Holy shit!! -Get me the fuck outta here!!"

TWIN FLAME:

"Oh, my Melinda, you remember!! -Look, myself and your guides, including Archangel Michael want to save you but you have to let at least one of us in first. There's absolutely no way we can enter that realm because you're heavily guarded by King Paimon by Satan's orders…"

ME:
"Realm? -What realm??"

TWIN FLAME:
"HELL. ...Melinda, you're in a HELL realm -but we're going to get you out!"

It was then I heard from Archangel Michael and a few other Angels and they told me to describe to them where I was, and they were going to do everything they could to get me out. What they revealed was I was within Satan's headquarters where King Paimon was babysitting me until Satan had ahold of me. I had no idea that Satan was this serious about capturing my own life but to face it at this level was unlike anything I ever could've ever imagined. My fear was at an all-time high, horrified I'd never see my daughters again, or even remember who I was. The fact that King Paimon had this much power over me only left me utterly speechless with paralyzed fear.

It took time for them to appear to rescue me, for there were many levels of this tower of hell I was in, similar to like different realms of hell. Describing that I was in the ninth floor from the very top where Lucifer resides.

But in order for me to be able to get them inside my direct doorway, I had to first battle the Demons that were keeping guard over me. That was the only way I could get them into the portal.

While at the same time, the Angels would be going through other routes in hopes to find a weak spot of protection the realm had in keeping souls from entering or leaving without permission of Lucifer.

The issue was I had absolutely no confidence after what I had been subjected to and the Angels knew this. Archangel Michael said with care that I had to have faith in myself to fight them, but I didn't have the strength after the energy depletion that King Paimon had drained.

That was when Archangel Michael decidedly shared his Divine power by transferring it me to fight the Demons out while I waited for them to get through the barrier.

Angels and other ascended beings are able to share their abilities temporarily with others to give them support, confidence and healing. When his power was merged with mine, I felt like a superwoman -*literally*. I suddenly had so much confidence in confronting Paimon's henchmen while at the same time able to see their weaknesses.

When I fought the Demons, it was surreal. I could feel every impact as the entangled cosmic warfare of good vs evil was in session. Demons were aware then that I had gotten into contact with Archangel Michael and knew that I had suddenly received his benevolent power of command. Once they could see my aura change, and manifest into another entity that ignited a golden white light through my soul vibration, that was when the resistance began.

Fighting Demons can be fun, I won't say it isn't a bit exhilarating - but the danger is no less real and isn't wise to take for granted for each moment is determined by your wave of thoughts, feelings, and the next move. Being a Sagittarius and a fire sign, it's in my nature to fight for what's right and for what I believe in. During this experience I felt my soul vibration become stronger and more in alignment of my passion.

I always dreamt as a little girl that I was surrounded by Angels and fighting evil for humanity. And so, you can imagine this experience suddenly becoming my reality as my soul mended with the one Archangel that I've dreamt and trusted the most. To even describe this is nearly impossible in human words, except to say… it was fucking AWESOME.

To misdirect my initial response of the minion Demon kings, they immediately shapeshifted to larger, broader and advanced beings that suddenly became an eye sore. Much was happening in this battle and I indeed had endured injuries that were excruciating.

The weapons in the other realms such as swords, knifes, axes and other types are charged with an electric power surge that enables the entity to deplete, stun, or even destroy ones enemy into pieces temporarily. When Demons attack living humans, it can cause the person to become severely mentally, emotionally unstable, physically ill, injured, or worse…**KILLED**.

At the exact time I had defeated the Demons that were keeping guard, I rushed to the portal and allowed my guides, Twin Flame and Archangel Michael in.

Thankfully however, I was guided through the entire battle with the Angels and my most trusted of spirit guides. Without them, I wouldn't be here with a sound mind (even though most would suggest otherwise).

As a Psychic Medium and a Demonologist, I've encountered so many entities that it's impossible to keep count. Though negatively overwhelming at times, it's granted me the ability to ascend past certain levels of fear and doubt within myself. When a soul reaches this level and has escalated to one that is then considered modestly advanced, they can fight Demons on the Astral Realm. This is what I'm capable of doing and I use this ability to help my clients. Although it's in our soul vibration to be courageous, that doesn't mean we don't face fear. No matter how far one ascends, no matter how fearless one becomes or how powerful one transcends, doesn't mean they are invincible. Even Angels possess times of weakness and call on each other for support.

True power comes in the form of friendship, trust, loyalty, teamwork, truth, and passion directed by a moral compass through the heart. Without these emotions inside, one cannot battle evil. This is the most humbling and invaluable lesson I've been gifted, and it's granted me a stronger spirit in remaining faithful in times of adversity.

LATER I DISCOVERED THE BEAUTIFUL NECKLESS THAT KING PAIMON HAD GIFTED ME, WAS IN FACT A CHAIN TO ENSLAVE MY SOUL. ARCHANGELS HAD TO USE HIGHLY EVOLVED WEAPONS TO BREAK THE SOULFUL SLAVERY.

BATTLE OF PRINCIPAL

I couldn't write this book without giving you a taste of this Demon encounter that I surely wish had never occurred.

It was late 2019, and I was just in the middle of writing this book while listing off the topics and subjects for it's contents. While doing this, I was also reading, *The Goetia of Solomon the King* as mentioned prior. I was reading the book because I had been receiving countless requests from fans to give my two cents on what I thought of the book and if any of the Demons were legit.

I hadn't read the book for more than a few pages before going to bed. When I stopped reading and put the book away and laid down to sleep, I suddenly awoke again in my room thinking I was physically awake. This experience was so real that it would've fooled **ANYONE**. As I sat up in my bed, I heard three knocks on my bedroom door. The space was completely mute with no sound whatsoever, but regardless, I went to the door and slowly opened it. To my bewilderment, I was taken aback when I came face to face with a massive demonic entity that reached close to my ceiling holding what appeared to be a weapon charged with immeasurable apathy.

Allow me to give you a glimpse into my first thought, which was - Oh **FUCK!!** -that was my initial response. Not only was I frightened that he was there, I had known immediately just by looking at him that he was one of the highest Demon lords. Afraid of doing frankly anything at all that could piss him off, I intuitively remained calm (this was extremely difficult), and asked him who he was…

ME:
"…Hello. May I ask who you are Demon?"

DEMON:
"…I HAVE SEVERAL NAMES, BUT YOUR KIND WOULD KNOW ME BETTER AS THE ONE AND ONLY BAEL."

BAEL is most commonly known as the First Principal Spirit King of the East that is in command and ruler of 66 legions of Demons mentioned in the *Lesser Key of Solomon*, written by *S.L. Macgregor Mathers* and *Aleister Crowley*…

ME:
"I see. I must thank you for being so forthcoming and respectful in knocking upon my door. Most Demons are not that way…"

BAEL:
"I AM NOT LIKE OTHER DEMONS. I DO NOT COME HERE TO FIGHT NOR TO BRING UPON WAR. I AM HERE BY MY MASTER'S COMMAND TO LET YOU KNOW THAT WE WILL BE ARRIVING TO YOU, AND I AM THE FIRST OF MANY. -FOR YOU ARE READING ABOUT US ARE YOU NOT?"

ME:
"…Yes. I have just begun to read the text, though I wasn't sure what to expect."

BAEL:
"AND NOW…?"

ME:
"Now…I have no doubt in your existence my lord on any account. I am in fact stricken with amazement at how astoundingly ferocious

you stand at my door. I have no doubt that you are not one to undermine."

BAEL:
"MY MASTER MENTIONED HOW WELL VERSED YOU ARE IN YOUR KNOWLEDGE OF US, AND SAID YOU TOO HAVE AN ABILITY OF YOUR OWN. HUMANS ARE NOT SO WISE WHEN SPEAKING TO MY KIN OR KNOW HOW TO HANDLE THEMSELVES IN COMBAT, BUT YOU'VE GAINED GREAT ATTENTION FROM MY LEAGUE..."

ME:
"...So, you *do* talk about me?... May I ask why? -I am nothing of a threat to you or your kin. In fact, I've always been confused as to why you or any Demon would attempt to silence me."

Bael's demonic figure practically overtook the entire hall. He appeared black with a monstrous face with horns at the top of his head. Spikes lingered along nearly his entire body as I too took notice of what appeared to be a large long tail that dragged heavy on the floor as if belonging to a dragon.

BAEL:
"OH, WE TALK ABOUT MANY HUMANS THAT THINK SO HIGHLY ABOUT THEMSELVES. IT'S NOT EVERY CENTURY WE ENCOUNTER A WOMAN DEMONOLOGIST THAT HAS ENOUGH COURAGE TO TAKE ON MY KIN."

ME:
"This is true. I have recognized the soul population, human and beast alike, to be alarmed by my profession of choice. But I do this not for thyself, but to help those that cannot help themselves. It isn't a mystery that many Demons attack even children without mercy and it's my Lightworker and Demonologist's oath to bring them to justice."

BAEL:
"JUSTICE? YOU THINK THAT BATTLING MY LEGIONS OR MYSELF IS JUSTICE? HUMAN GIRL, YOU HAVE MUCH TO LEARN. IT IS NOT JUSTICE YOU DO THIS FOR, YOU DO THIS FOR YOUR PRIDE AND EGO..."

ME:
"You're wrong. Yes, I do enjoy the satisfactory of reclaiming my own higher self, but I am at my prime of energetic vibration when my heart is put to the test. And as long as I am here, and in existence, my

purpose will be to bring a new line of **Lightwarriors** to protect our own -even against you and your kin."

Bael wasn't happy when I made this known. I can still remember the sound of his hoarse voice. A stampede of grisly discomfort shot through my soul as he spoke. He began to snarl as he raised his weapon up to my line of sight…

BAEL:
"SUCH BOLD WORDS COMING FROM A HUMAN GIRL -A GIRL THAT IS ALONE…"

UNKNOWN VOICE:
"-She's not alone."

Upon hearing this familiar voice, both Bael and my gaze turned to see Joshua (Yehoshua in Hebrew) sitting quietly at the foot of the stairs a distance in the hall. He stood and slowly walked my way and suddenly I felt like I could breathe again. (We don't breathe on the Astral Realm FYI).

BAEL:
"…JOSHUA. I SEE YOU'RE HERE TO DEFEND THIS…DEMONOLOGIST. WHAT DO YOU THINK?

...Does she have what it takes in combat?"

Joshua (Yehoshua):

"We meet again Bael… and yes, I've seen her with my own eyes. She's quite gifted with a sword. But we're not here for war, as you've said…right?"

Bael winced at the word, war, as Joshua stood between me and the oversized otherworldly malevolence.

Some people would be surprised to know that Yehoshua prefers to be called Joshua, so as to keep it simple for those that believe, follow or have heard of him. It's not in Joshua's nature to be arrogant nor does he challenge Demons. It's come to my understanding with extensive personal time with him that he's much into peace with the entities but will defend one against another if necessary. He is considered an **Ascended Master** but would never say so if you met him, for he's more focused on you and your needs. When he knew that I was working on my book, he has been keeping a close eye on me and I'm eternally grateful.

When Joshua appeared, he was wearing casual clothes like anyone else. His style of clothing, hair and chosen physical appearance has altered as earth style changes so as to remain in the same likeness of living humans. This way, it helps those he encounters in dreams or on the astral realm to feel comfortable of his visitation.

If a person that he visits, pictures him as a specific image from a religious view or other means, he may approach them as what the person expects, to eliminate confusion or fear of deception. His biggest passion is people, and to make them feel comfortable, valued and safe as much as possible.

I remember Joshua standing next to me exceptionally clear as day, almost as if it happened on earth just yesterday. His presence is one I admire probably the most out of all souls when it comes to soulful mastery and internal betterment through one's experiences and lessons. Standing beside me, gently he took my hand to help me feel secure while in the presence of what hell had brought to my door. The very touch from his hand nearly made me blush. Soft to the touch yet one could sense his undeniable stance in command over the Demon's unexpected intrusion. I could feel his energy begin blending within mine, and it led me to wonder if his intention to protect me in love and concern wasn't of just as a guide…

As Bael remained standing in my hallway late in the night, I knew that Lucifer hadn't sent him just for casual plight. Thoughts arose and I knew that perhaps this could be my chance to show Bael and his master what I'm made of. It's not in my usual attitude to be confrontational, but on the other realms, there's another side of me that is of higher vibration that is in absolute devotion of making my mark on where I stand…

ME:
"Joshua, can I talk to you alone for a second…?"

As we walked a distance from Bael for private conversation, that's when Joshua reminded me that we can have private talks through telepathy…

JOSHUA (YEHOSHUA):
"How are you holding up? I can sense your fear is high. You mustn't be afraid Melinda. I won't let him hurt you. He knows I can put him in his place if he tried anything."

ME:
"I am fearful that's for sure, but I know this is going to sound foolish, but I feel like I should spar him…"

JOSHUA (YEHOSHUA):
"I wouldn't recommend it Melinda. He's the first Demon in command next to Lucifer and he fights **DIRTY**, I know this from years of experience. He's not one to go into battle with. -He won't be easy on you because you're a woman. His way is to inflict pain and suffering and will use all of his power against you. It wouldn't be a fair fight…"

ME:
"I know this sounds foolish, but somewhere within my soul I feel like I have to do this. Everything happens for a reason, and the universe chose -they chose to come here. The universe wouldn't have brought him if I wasn't ready for this experience. I feel as if I need to learn more and fighting him will expand my abilities."

I then looked at Bael and willingly approached him…

ME:
"Oh, great and powerful Bael, leader of fear, soldier of hell and keeper of legions… I'd like to challenge you to a duel. Not for the purpose of winning or losing, but as a learning experience. Without your Demons or legions interfering -just you and I. Do you except?"

The great King of hell widened his eyes in excitement from the unexpected spar opportunity. He did not hesitate as he leaned over my short stature and replied…

BAEL:
"YOU'RE EITHER VERY BRAVE, OR FOOLISH... BUT I ACCEPT..."

Me:
"And don't hold back just because I'm a woman."

Bael:
"It is not in my nature of mercy. You know this don't you female demonologist...?"

Let's just say I was given another chance at learning how powerful I can be as long as I have faith in me. It was held in my hallway outside of my bedroom on the astral realm and felt all so real. Too real. So surreal that my astral body felt heavy as if gravity still had a hold of me. There were times where I felt like I was going to lose this fight, for Bael was most certainly cruel on every level imaginable. He left no amount of empathy as he and I fought. His otherworldly strength surpassed mine on an extremely high level that I was injured most unexpectedly. There's no shy way of saying it -he was kicking my ass. His ability to shield himself was all so new to me. Even Joshua had warned me that Bael possessed powers beyond my capabilities, but I knew I had to at least try.

It didn't take long until I was slammed to the floor so hard, I felt as if several bones had broken. Joshua knew I wanted to do this, but he never left and always said I could get out of it whenever I wanted. But I didn't want to give up. I refused to quit and wanted to make a name for myself. For Bael and the rest of his kin to know who I am, and what I believe in.

It was more than just a fight. It was a statement to the rest of the Demons in the universe. I knew that if they were going to talk about me, then I wanted it to be about my power. I wanted them to begin to fear me, fear my name, fear my presence and overall soulful ability to transcend the fuck out of anyone that crosses those I love and care about. I may not sound like your typical Lightworker, but that's because I'm *not*. I'm a Lightwarrior, and that's exactly what I knew I had to announce to this Demon and to the rest of them.

It was in my deepest thoughts that I heard Archangel Michael say in telepathy, that I must have faith in myself. He guided me in learning how to hold my power within myself on an energetic and soulful level. Reminding me that a soul without love as their guiding source will not win, but parish. When a soul faces adversity, they should remain in a presence of absolute focus at all times of their own thoughts and emotions. As long as one is in full control of how they feel about themselves, they will be able to overcome any obstacle that lay before them.

Slammed on the ground from my lack in faith and confidence in myself. The more insecure I got, the less power I could harvest, thus making it an easier win for my foe. Thanks to both Joshua and Archangel Michael, they gave me a chance in redeeming myself with their help. I cannot take all of the credit, for they have given me more support than I can relay.

With his help, I was able to borrow energy from the universe and Archangel Michael to recharge myself. Internally I could feel a difference in my vibrational pulse that which enabled my higher self to emerge. Like my soul had suddenly took a universal vitamin full of righteous supplements. Replenished as if from drinking from the water of life, raised to my feet once more, and within a swift twirl I transitioned. Changing my form from a warrior to a Goddess full of love, light and wrath. Each form one chooses to take will be based on one's mood, much like a mood ring. And it was here I made the Demon know of who I was and how I would command it to leave. When Bael could see my full potential he fought harder, faster and became even larger. But I wasn't afraid, nor was I willing to allow it to stay in my home. After several minutes confronting this entity, I did things to him that not even I am proud of, and for that I won't say. -Except that at the end before I threw him out, I cut off his male appendage and shoved it violently down his throat. Told him to never come to my home again unannounced and banished him out with a Godly smite.

No one is immune to fear, pain and suffering and will never truly be impenetrable. The refusal to give up is what keeps the soul ascending, transforming and recharging one's ability to continue in the face of adversity. It's not in one's power of talent but in the power of one's mind that makes one a worthy foe, healer or hero.

DEVIL'S HOUSE

For *Ghost Adventures* fans, I'm certain this part is one you'll most enjoy but it's one that I've not favored since watching this documentary. When the *Demon House* documentary was released in 2018 by *Zak Bagans*, the Lead Paranormal Investigator, producer and host of *Ghost Adventures* on *Travel Channel*, it became one of most the talked about in terms of the paranormal community.

Zak Bagans has been known to outdo himself on numerous occasions with taunting Demons, spirits, including Devil entities. I've grown rather fond of his determination to continue to expose Demons and familiar spirits of their agenda towards humanity and how to guard oneself from these malicious otherworldly fiends. However not as impressed nor in support in times when he or one of his crew members will challenge an entity or conduct a ritual that was not thought through first.

I get why they challenge spirits. To get the entity to become irate so as to gather paranormal evidence, but eventually it comes at a great price and usually not one can soulfully afford.

When I first heard about *Demon House*, I wanted to watch it because I knew intuitively that Zak's skills in documentary film making was going to be delivered as raw as possible. But it was also why I delayed watching it for over a year after it was initially released. I knew there would be a risk if I watched it. Somehow, deep down I knew that it could get bad and fast and with that in mind I delayed it as long as I could. However, it didn't take long for my amazing and supportive fans to ask me repeatedly nearly on a daily basis if I would review *Demon House*.

Reviewing *Demon House* wasn't a challenge, it was the fact that the moment I watched the film, suddenly I felt a heavy thick shadow figure standing directly behind me. I was watching it on YouTube as a rental purchase, and when I began to watch it while making notes at the same time, I would feel a massive cold chill in the room. Not to forget my head started hurting from unexpected head pains as if someone had struck my skull several times. These weren't normal headaches either, these head pains were as if someone was intentionally stabbing one part of my brain with a long sharp object. It would get so painful I had to pause just to take over the counter pain medicine to alleviate it. But the cold was still hovering over me, and the overshadowing figure remained as it stood, behind me and wouldn't leave.

About an hour into the documentary, I then saw what appeared to be like a tall entity with horns that were sharp and curled in my third eye. The face was long and goat-like, or similar to a bull and draped in a long black cloak. It must've been nearly nine feet tall. This sucker was **BIG**, and its presence not only disturbed my level of thought the entire time watching the film but implanted severe anxiety and panic attacks for hours afterward.

When I was done watching the documentary and had gone to bed,

WORD OF ADVICE:
DON'T WATCH THIS AT NIGHT!

-I then dreamt and found myself on the astral realm standing in my family's living room and there staring back at me was the same Demon from the documentary.

-No shit, not kidding, not exaggerating, the

SAME DEMON WAS STANDING IN FRONT
OF ME FROM THE FILM!

I not only was beside myself in shock -*but I was literally there beside myself alone!?* The entity had somehow known I was watching the film to review to help people be warned of his existence and he was pissed!

Out of all of the entities I've come to face, he was one of the

MOST AGGRESSIVE

Demons I've ever encountered.

The longer I was in this entity's presence the more I began to detect it's rank. Eventually I was informed by the Demon that its closely related to the rank of becoming a Devil level. The Demon rank it upholds is one of power and control over several legions of other Demons. The entity controls many types of forces and can command Demons to do it's bidding.

THE DEMON EVENTUALLY TOLD ME HIS NAME, AND HE SAID HIS NAME IS **ASTAROTH**. THIS IS AN ACTUAL DEMON MENTIONED IN DEMONOLOGY AS THE GREAT DUKE OF HELL IN THE FIRST HIERARCHY WITH BEELZEBUB AND LUCIFER. HE IS A PART OF THE EVIL TRINITY.

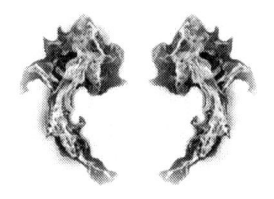

When I was facing the Demon, he had spoken in a voice that can only be described as the vibration that only hell would love. It truly was one of the most notable entities to avoid at all costs! Was I afraid? Are you kidding? **-OF COURSE I WAS AFRAID!** -I nearly shit my astral pants!

Remaining serious at best, I knew that the Demon feeds on fear and I had to remain as focused as humanly and psychicly possible within my own thoughts. The power of a Demon lies within their ability to sew negative thoughts into the victims. Plainly, the entity only has the power over you if you give it to them but the Demon's ability to uphold that level of evil was especially tactful. The very steps it took could awaken the bravest of souls from their cribs in the night. It never deterred from eye contact and there was even a moment we had exchanged words…

ASTAROTH:
"I HEAR YOU'RE WATCHING THE DOCUMENTARY ABOUT ME. AM I WHAT YOU IMAGINED?"

ME:
"More…"

The demon began to chuckle with pride of his overpowering presence. The very vibration of his voice caused each shiver within me to triple…

ASTAROTH:
"…WHAT IS IT ABOUT ME THAT MAKES YOU SHAKE? I HEAR YOU'RE A WORTHY ADVERSARY FOR A HUMAN -NO LESS

FOR A WOMAN. IMPRESSIVE...BUT FOOLISH..."

ME:
"Most Demonologists are men -true. But I plan to change that. Not to disrespect your stellar impressive rank, but to enlighten others of your existence so as to remain wise in such encounters with respect..."

ASTAROTH:
"INDEED. MEN HAVE ENCOUNTERED ME AND REGRETTED IT. RESPECT IS DUE FOR YOU HUMANS ARE NEITHER POWERFUL NOR ABLE TO DO WHAT I CAN DO."

ME:
"I know you're more than capable of much. But may I ask, what are you capable of? May I know your rank so as to know the grace of your presence with full dignity?"

I've learned after many encounters with Demons that it's wise to stay humble, at least in the beginning. It's not smart to disrespect an entity you're not sure of. With this respect he remained calm and spoke with high pride and ego which distracted the Demon for Angels to show up in due time...

ASTAROTH:
"I AM ONE OF THE HIGHEST RANKS BUT THERE ARE MANY OTHERS ABOVE ME. I AM CONSIDERED A DUKE IN MY RANK..."

Talking with the Demon wasn't easy for each time I attempted to speak it would linger so close to me that I could smell it's breath. Surprisingly the stench of this Demon was not rotten at all but instead smelled of flowers. When I mentioned how pleasant he smelt, he said it didn't like to smell foul but something pleasant to entice humans. Even he had a level of distinction that could be considered class. Regardless of how good he smelt, it didn't bombard my senses from knowing he was a Demon in seek of human souls. His intention to seek mine wasn't on his agenda but he made to mention that mine is one he wouldn't mind obtaining considering the hit list I was on…

ASTAROTH:
"...ARE YOU NOT AWARE THAT I COULD KILL YOU RIGHT NOW?"

ME:
"Oh, I'm very much aware of your royal ability. And I thank you for telling me of your respectable rank. I am grateful."

ASTAROTH:
"...YOU KNOW THAT I COULD KILL YOU EASILY IF I CHOOSE YET YOU STAND HERE IN COMPLIMENT. I CAN SEE YOU SPOKEN TO MANY DEMONS. YOU KNOW YOUR PLACE. MOST HUMANS DO NOT ADDRESS US WITH SUCH GRACE."

ME:
"I've had many unforgettable and painful experiences from your kind. None that I can say were pleasant -but unforgettable, nonetheless. But, as respectable I shall be in your presence, being below you is neither my place nor humanity's. This is your ego speaking…"

ASTAROTH:
"DO YOU CHALLENGE MY AUTHORITY?!!"

With a quicken step the goat faced Demon growled as he stood now only a few inches from my face.

ME:
"I do not. Only stating what is the truth. We are not below you, nor are we bound by you. You have no authority over me or humanity."

DEMON DEALER

Astaroth:
"We'll see about that?!..."

And with that, Astaroth took a heavy step backward as his two hoofs for feet collided with the floor in a roar. Motioning his body as he inhaled what looked like dark energy circulating around him similar to stardust that shined like glitter. Beautiful at first but rapidly transformed him into a hideous monster with a face only a Demon mother could love. His eyes full of madness immediately changing from black to a pulsating red with small darts for pupils. His hair became spiked that curved to an arch like crooked tree branches.

Within seconds I could hear what seemed like hundreds of different types of Demon laughter surrounding me in this horrid space that I once called home. Astaroth announced to his legions that I was now his enemy and was going to show me just how much authority he had.

Before I could do anything, the demon ordered two of his most loyal of followers to hold me still as he then mutated into something so horrifying that I just remember shaking in fear as tears flooded my eyes. The sound of broken bones snapping and breaking as his body adjusted in the most violent stream of disturbia and mayhem. I watched as more arms burst from his sides along with a long tail that matched one of a dragons whipping in a violent snap. Without hesitation the duke of hell hunched over his stature as spikes gruesomely pierced through his spine, arms, shoulders, face and legs.

Blood exploded from the exposed skin and dripped down the inhuman physique. Following two massive horns breaking through his skull to announce his power of plenty as he began dancing in what then manifested a ring of fire. Legions upon legions gave way through portals as hundreds shuffled savagely in the wake of the newly procession of what now I've determined was my soon possession.

I could hardly fathom on what I was witnessing. In desperation, I repeated the words, "*It's just a dream*", in my mind hoping none of this was real. Not only terrifying but made me feel like I was literally looking into fear's soul and presence. I felt completely alone and helpless. And though I tried to fight back the fear it was too overpowering that my energy was being depleted rapidly, to the point that my own soul's energy was losing strength by seconds.

Demons pounding on the skin created drums began to sound off a rhythm of doom. Drumming and chanting began to circulate around me as I watched the hundreds of dreaded creatures feast upon human flesh.

Astaroth could not only see but read into my very soul's mind and declared…

ASTAROTH:
"THIS IS NOT A DREAM. AND YOU ARE NOT GOING TO ESCAPE."

Trying with all of my might to speak, shakenly I asked…

ME:
"…Is… Is this what you do when you possess someone?"

Laughter overthrew the ambience echoing the entire now hell arena. Flames of burning flesh consumed my senses as the chatter tickled their egos of my ignorance. Astaroth roared a mighty bellow in his hellish temple as he revealed to what I never thought my mind would painstakingly hear…

ASTAROTH:
"YOU DON'T KNOW? I THOUGHT YOU KNEW EVERYTHING MY QUEEN… NO, THIS IS WHAT WE DO WHEN WE ARE GOING TO TAKE YOU INTO ME…"

UNKNOWN VOICE:
"-NO!! SHE'S MINE!!!"

Quake of dread dealt the ground, the atmosphere and within as the unknown voice of what I assumed was greater authority over Astaroth. Glancing up at the circulation of Demons that once surrounded me in a hell ring, all began to run in fear. Knowing that

Demons rarely fear anything, I knew from their own reaction that this meant serious trouble (not that I wasn't in trouble already).

Impending doom overtook my entire soul vibration as a portal of fire appeared out of thin air and a giant beast unlike anything I've ever seen slowly emerged through the portal. First a large foot then a leg and the rest of the unforgiveable guise of desecration climbed out of the underworld portal.

It was here, in this exact moment that I knew I was in the presence of none other than **SATAN** himself.

As if he's done this all day with my kind, Satan sat upon a thrown massed with skulls and just looked at me and began saying words fueled in negativity. No conversation this time. He would just say horrible mean disgusting ruthless things and each verbal attack began to feel sharp like knives in my head, astral body and my place of love. This may seem simple to fight but it was unlike any other attack I've encountered. With each word or phrase, he would shout, whisper or say, would use his power to harm me as a violent attack. This was like a physical attack with words. A mental and verbal attack gone physical. The words would begin to cut my very body and cause my own soul energy to drift towards him as he gladly inhaled it into him. The more cuts, the more my own energy was seeping out of my astral body and would float towards him as if I was slowly dissipating energetically. The more he inhaled and took in a piece of me, I began to feel as if I was losing a sense of my very entirety…

SATAN:
"DO YOU FEEL THAT...? ...YOUR VERY EXISTENCE FADING INTO ME? SOON THERE WON'T BE ANYTHING LEFT OF YOU AND NO ONE IS HERE TO SAVE YOU..."

Negative thoughts swarmed inside me uncontrollably. Things like why I couldn't understand why no one would keep me safe. My heart, my spirit felt broken in this moment. I couldn't understand why even Angels wouldn't rescue me now, or when I was raped. He would shout how much of a loser I was and how no one in their right mind would love me. Shouting that I deserved what I got in my past and how I don't have any power at all. All of the pain I've ever endured was in this moment. All I could hear was him telling me I was worthless, useless, hopeless, weak, a waste of existence.

Crying and begging for the entity to have mercy as I tried to shut my eyes, I then heard Archangel Michael in telepathy reminding me that I had to remember it was all lies.

ARCHANGEL MICHAEL:
"Melinda. Don't listen to him! He is a liar and will say anything to make you feel bad about yourself. I'm here, you don't have to worry anymore. -But you must be brave and don't let him win! It's all in your faith in yourself. Don't let his lies change or alter how you feel about yourself."

ME:

"Why aren't you or anyone here?"

I asked sobbingly in despair…

ARCHANGEL MICHAEL:

"I am trying to get to you, but you must remember your God Particle Melinda. You've fought Demons before, and I believe in you!"

ME:

"What can I do? I'm just a small human. I can't do anything right! I can't even stop a man from raping me! Satan is right Michael, I can't ever do anything right, why would anyone love me. Why would you care?!"

ARCHANGEL MICHAEL:

"Dear Melinda…what happened to you was never your fault and Satan is using the pain to hurt you. You must know by now that I love you and care about you. You're very special and have so much ability to help so many people. What makes you so special is how much you care for humanity. Your heart is what makes you special. You're far from a loser Melinda. Lucifer knows this and that's why he appeared to you. But you must remember you're stronger than him for within you is a light that he doesn't have. You need to have faith in yourself and to shine your light from within…"

Archangel Michael then quickly appeared with other benevolent beings from a rainbow light portal and fought Satan. Hunter and my Twin Flame both appeared from the same portal and grabbed me in care to shelter me from further despair. It didn't take the Angels long to cast Satan out and the demon with his legions but even I was amazed at how much of a battle this moment was. Archangels are exceptionally powerful in battle and have abilities I've not seen in other Angels before. And even they relied on each other in absolute faith to banish the unholy.

Once Satan and his legions were casted out, Angels went around the land to secure it with protections that one may suggest were like a spell. There is a power to Angels but most of the time Angels rarely show their true abilities because many humans would fear it so. But I knew this was their genuine side of livelihood that not only impressed me but inspired me for further self-discovery of my own unique power.

After Archangel Michael and the others rescued me, I later was informed that I was in a spiritual soul battle. What Archangel Michael explained in this moment was I had experienced a part of a **SOUL STEALING RITUAL** that Demons partake in order to condemn human souls.

I cannot thank the Angels enough for what they did for me. It's still a haunting experience that has caused me to become emotional just writing this for you. Writing, sharing and documenting my own astral experiences has been difficult but it's allowed me the chance to heal and to evolve further to self-acceptance.

Archangel Michael and Angels... thank you for all eternity
♥

THE OATH

BIRTH OF A DEMON DEALER

I was twenty-six years old when these horrific encounters started to occur, and each experience lingers in my memory as if it happened only yesterday. The haunting never truly stops when one is faced with pure evil. You never are the same again. Something changes in you. A deep-rooted change that alters one state of being, an understanding and even respect for evil.

You begin to learn and accept that evil comes in all shapes and sizes and only continues to grow as long as we allow it or don't at least ask for help from the otherworldly benevolence. You no longer look at people and situations the same way anymore. What you once thought was frightening or scary, eventually turns into another obstacle one must face and overcome.

Even a casual conversation with a stranger can turn into another demonic attack from an unclean influence that instilled into the person that I encounter. I'll sense the entity, even speak to it on the astral realm while still partaking my usual human tasks. But none would be the wiser unless able to see through my Psychic encounters. And the more my abilities grew, the more I developed a sense of seeing and hearing the entities rather profoundly to the point where it was impossible to ignore -and impossible to escape.

People ask why I got into Demonology in the first place, but the truth is, I didn't go looking for Demons, they came looking for me. From what Demons have revealed is they were attacking me to stop me from becoming a Demonologist, but all it did was anger me more. Intensifying the urge to help the people I was guiding and reading, felt that it was my universal duty and cosmic responsibility to help those that couldn't help themselves.

How can I say no to helping someone with a Demon that's attacking their five-year old child? How can I simply just ignore the fact a Demon is raping your wife at night in her sleep? How does one simply turn a blind eye as a shadow crawls on to your bed, climbs on top of you and puts you in sleep paralysis? -How could anyone just ignore that type of apathetic paranormal phenomenon? -Could you?

It was inevitable that the more I opened myself up to the benevolent side of the spirit realm, the more I was attacked by the malevolent entities. No warnings, just constant, mindless and merciless bashing from Demons and other negative forces. The attacks became ever so frequent that I expected it as a part of my nightly routine and eventually a daily one. And the more I was trying to help someone from their own paranormal happenings, the more I experienced what they were going through and how unbearable it was. I could feel every emotion, every ounce of fear and panic my clients were going through and their families. And the more I endured their pain, the more I wanted to save them from it.

As the attacks merged with my life, I slowly adjusted and transitioned into it like a chameleon that changes form. Eventually strengthening my abilities and mindset to what would be identified much like a warrior spirit.

I made a promise to myself years into this that if I was going to be a Demonologist, I wasn't going to just read about it. I wasn't going to just listen to stories, and I most certainly wasn't going to run from it when it knocked on my door -*literally*. Making the decision that I was going to make sure Demons and Devils KNEW my name, and that I wasn't going to stop fighting for others. As long as they kept haunting and terrorizing people, I was going to do whatever it took to help others from otherworldly maliciousness.

A Demonologist's Life Lesson

When I decided to become a Demonologist, it was stomach turning because I knew that it would get dark fast. I knew that by opening that doorway of cosmic truth of malevolent entities, that I wouldn't be able to shut it. But it was from a deep passion to help people that led me to be brave enough to do so. It's never easy doing the right thing because if it was, then a lot of people would do it.

Many people become a Demonologist for the wrong reasons and think it's something to brag about. But when they go into it, you'll notice many of them regret it and won't ever go down that road again. I don't blame them. Becoming a Demonologist isn't about studying Demons to look like some paranormal badass. If that's why you want to study demonology, then you will get a **RUDE AWAKENING** my friend.

The study of Demonology is a collection of cosmic ancient malevolent entity information that's roughly been all too generalized. The more I read into many demonology texts, the more I realized people were writing on how to summon and control Demons and Devils of a certain rank. Just by reading through several books I found myself enraged over the lack of knowledge and common sense of these authors. I knew it wouldn't be long before I'd begin writing my own and for the *right* reasons.

As a Demonologist my life gets turned upside down on a daily basis due to the constant uninvited guests like Bael. Just a few nights ago I had gone to sleep and suddenly felt a very large invisible force pull my body out of my bed on the astral realm and pull me up to the ceiling. Though I tried to kick it and do whatever I could, it practically stunned my abilities and I was just a human in this moment. Helpless and unable to defend myself, the entity spread my legs, pulled off my clothes, shoved my face into the bed and began to rape me.

Demons and Devils rape their victims, especially women, with the intention to dehumanize and tear down the divine feminine energy. This is one of the most powerful ways to hurt women due to the amount of immense helplessness as a female energy when she is being attacked in a way that makes her feel worthless and helpless. The Divine male and female energies represent different aspects in themselves that make them unique. When Demons attack, they do so by triggering the notion of what it is factual in the representation of the soul energy and what that individual fears the most. Because I've been a survivor of rape and other levels of sexual abuse in my life, Demons prey on that in attempt to destroy my will to carry on.

This was the entity's attempt to scare me away from my purpose to enlighten and empower you. It's not the first time I've had a

Demon do this to me, and probably won't be the last. Admittedly, I was frightened while being degraded once again to the point of having to heal once more. Each attack attempt from a negative spirit is a personal one because that's exactly how they intend it. It's meant to derail you from your immediate focus so as to challenge your ability to push you into a darkened path of emotions.

But what this Demon and other entities forget is as they have their mission, so do I. And it would appear that his mission had failed and mine perseveres.

The general public would rather smell the roses of ignorance than bear the scars of reality. People are too frightened to hear the word **DEMON**, let alone research them. I understood this for I used to also be frightened of the entities very existence that I'd cringe just hearing the name of one. However, overtime I began to realize that fear of the very name gave the entity power due to the fear that was manifesting from inside of my thoughts and emotions. **FEAR** is what Demons feed off of and it was from this simple understanding, that gave me back a little bit of my power.

And the more I endured horrendous demonic attacks the stronger I became. I began to learn things about them and understand their way of deception. I started to get braver and less frightened by the things they would do to scare me. And because of this, they were having more of a challenge of making me reluctant to do anything that is meant to empower humans against them.

A Lightwarrior's Heart

Most folks are taught to believe that it's heresy to suggest in any sort of way, that humans could potentially be all powerful like a God, or like that of Angels. I used to believe this lie too. But I learned this lie was the worst lie the human race would come to believe, for that's exactly what the…

Devil wants you to believe!

For the more I grew into my world of demonological hauntings, I started to uncover it's raw reality -that **RELIGION IS WRONG.**

Arriving to the uncanny possibility that even religion was created by dark forces in order to not just control people, but to tarnish any level of humanity's cosmic power that's inside and has always been a part of humanity.

In the beginning when I would be attacked by Demons, I can openly say I was beyond terrified. I would lose sleep nearly every night and would refuse to even sleep alone in my own bedroom. I'd have to sleep in my daughter's room just to also make sure she wasn't alone if it was in the house.

But now, I prepare for battle on the other realms, and manifest myself into a **LIGHTWARRIOR**.

It's part of my ascension and if you've not heard of this, it's partially because people that have ascended this far are quiet because they don't like being called crazy. The other reason is because very few living souls will ascend to this level, but when they do, they are no longer the same in many ways.

The transition from LIGHTWORKER to a LIGHTWARRIOR, isn't for all Lightworkers. Few Lightworkers will transcend to Lightwarrior when they possess a pure fighting spirit that is driven to help bring justice and a universal balance for all that is good. Becoming a Lightwarrior, you make a divine oath inside of yourself (at least I have), to watch over humanity, help them when they need it, and to defend them when they deserve it. It's not in my nature to back away from a fight, and firmly believe in the depths of my soul that as long as there is love inside of us, it's always and forever worth protecting.

Though I may appear as if I am always in control of myself, my emotions or that I'm "okay" -doesn't mean I am. I've gotten rather skilled at faking a smile just so you don't know how much hell I've been dealing with. When I appear on camera there have been so many times where I didn't want to record due to crying. The astral experiences are indeed amazing and can be the best and most healing moments a soul can ever embrace. But there's a level that Demons can put a person so deep to the point where you cannot feel your own light anymore. You will feel as if you don't even know or trust yourself.

When I struggled with suicidal thoughts it was emotions from Demons and Devils inflicting the worst kind of pain possible. But when I could have crossed to that point of nearly no return, it was my Twin Flame, Hunter, Angels and Joshua that were there for me. And when they knew it would help, they would bring my departed precious daughter's soul, Victoria to visit me. Reminding me of how much love I have in myself, and how much I still have to offer. Their love, guidance and immense support has blessed me on more levels than I can possibly put into words. Reminding me on why I started this journey in the first place and why I **must** keep going.

But more importantly, that people I know love me, and that my beautiful amazingly talented daughter Josslyn who's still living, needs me just as much as I need her.

It would be a complete bullshit lie if I said that I have it handled all the time. Demons get into your mind *literally* making you think things and see things that can make a person go completely unhinged. I've feared of where my lightwork and demonology path could lead me. From utter exhaustion, pouring against the current of peace as the emotional tsunami was too much to contain. Merely in the shy year of 33, my soul has been through much toil. It takes a toll on me each time I face Demons and each time I go into battle. Marking, leaving a scar of eternal memory of what I've endured, sacrificed and surpassed. Coming at a high price that cannot be undone. It lingers in your physical body and can make one ill, or even die if not careful.

But because of my continual guidance from amazingly loving souls whom I wouldn't trade for anything, have taught me how strong I am by continuing to believe in myself. Because of them, they taught me the true meaning of what it means to love and honor others regardless of their mistakes and of their past. To live your life with dignity, respect and loyalty to yourself and then to others.

Without their immeasurable skills in healing, love, patience, protection and guidance…I wouldn't have known what it means to be empowered and to have faith in myself.

Their benevolent support, and impressive patience, is one of the most selfless gifts I could ever ask for. After so much already in this moment I knew that I had to trust in faith that this will all be worth it.

I never thought I'd be here today writing another book for you, nor did I ever imagine that I'd be where I am soulfully. Yet, after all that I've endured, I've been able to transcend into something that heals in her own way. We all have our own skills, talents, and abilities -this is mine and I wouldn't change it for anything. Not for all of the fame, money or any temporary item in this world, would I ever wish to alter the life I've lived.

A DEMONOLOGIST'S VOW

Though I wish I could sit here and tell you I'm indestructible, I'm obviously not. Working in this field of the paranormal comes with a torn and heavy heart. The work as a Demonologist creates chaos in one's thoughts, sleep, and daytime experiences. Demons also possess the ability to give one severe bad luck, ill health and can even bring negative experiences and bad people into your life without you even knowing it.

Having my Psychic abilities, I'm able to communicate with my guides and see what Demons are up to so as to be warned in advanced. This is a huge advantage. But I'm not perfect and can be tricked and deceived at times. No one is immune to the demonic warfare that may enter your space and take away your ability to defend yourself and those you love.

And knowing this truth, won't deter me from my focus and eternal oath I've made to myself and to humanity. In this oath, I made a promise to help guide and love humanity even if they didn't know I was there. Astrally I help people in their situations many times, but most will never know I was a part of their success, healing, guidance or protection. And that's okay. I don't do this for praise. I started and do this because I know what it's like feeling utterly helpless and completely alone.

MELINDA KAY LYONS

Now over the course of much training and after more experience than what is shared, I've been able to detain the situation if need be. Angels and other Lords of the Universe have indeed granted me a few careful selected weapons, including a sword and a tiara that shines upon my head. There are several of us Lightwarriors that have been slowly coming out of hiding to shed light on the gloomed path. For Demons and other malevolent forces are enraged over this understanding I've obtained and continue to disturb my soulful task.

THE FOREGOING SPIRITUAL WARFARE IS REAL AND IS HAPPENING ALL AROUND US EVERY DAY, BUT IT'S IN THE COMING OUT TO SHINE OUR LIGHT THAT WILL KEEP THE DARKNESS AT BAY.

My deepest and most precious wish is that I have ended someone's suffering from otherworldly spirits by empowering them to grow into stronger people and souls. Both the living and the dead are suffering every moment of everyday because of negative forces at work in the shadows. And it's become my absolute Lightworker and Lightwarrior mission to see to it that I not only help as many as I can, but enlighten them on the power they have inside. We're light beings that have tremendous power beyond basic human comprehension and this power can do more and enable more than one could literally dream of. Because of this power, Demons want to take that power away by sucking the life and existence out of each and every soul and keep it for themselves.

Writing this book didn't come from my imagination, nor was it just some "creative story" -I lived it. I lived it all. And each experience enabled me to learn and understand new aspects about myself that I never thought were possible. And as long as I'm still in existence…whether breathing oxygen or have transitioned to the other side -it will remain to be my SOULITARIAN mission to keep fighting the good fight, helping people and bringing souls to justice.

Based on all I hold authentic and from the soul of my own being…
this is based on a true story.

MELINDA KAY LYONS

ACKNOWLEDGEMENTS

This book couldn't have been written without the absolute protection, love, healing and guidance by my amazing spirit guides, Hunter, Joshua (Jesus), Twin Flame and the many benevolent Angels. Not to forget the pouring of light and love from the many other precious souls that I've encountered along the way.

I would like to thank the incredible support from my dad who's not only supported my work from the beginning but has granted me immeasurable advice that's guided me into wiser decisions. Including the love and support from my family that's believed in my dreams, hard work and have instilled further belief in myself.

I couldn't have gone through my darkest times without the immeasurable love and healing from my Twin Flame. You've not ceased to amaze me. Though we've gone through much sorrow, we always manage to overcome the dimmed moments and came out sparkling. Forever will my heart appreciate your sincere presence, humility, honesty, truth and overpowering love.

To my amazingly wonderfully precious daughters, Victoria and Josslyn. My heart and spirit couldn't have surpassed all that I've seen and endured if it wasn't for your memory and love to give me hope once more. Hope within myself, in a bright future and in the overindulgence of your joyful smiles. Thank you for allowing me to be your imperfect mother and giving me the chance to start again each day. I love you both more than words could ever describe, and it's with your images in my heart and mind that make me feel more alive.

To my incredible fans. I started this journey with a dream to help guide and assist others in their paranormal experiences. To inspire and to work my ass off in hopes that in the process my work shows where my heart lies. But the truth shall remain, it's because of your belief in me and in your generous love and support that's given me the strength and faith in myself to keep going when all light goes out.

Thank you for the haters and Demons. It's because of your doubt in me that I keep going, to show you how strong I can be.

ABOUT THE AUTHOR

MELINDA KAY LYONS was born in Alaska and raised in the Last Frontier for a majority of her life. She is a proud mother of two daughters.

Melinda does not align herself with religion but is in ultimate faith of the power of the universe, spirit and source of love.

As her years stretched after her near-death experience, so did her intuitiveness and divine abilities as a Psychic Medium. Thanks to many positive influences, and pushes in the right direction, her dream of healing others has become a reality.

As a Lightworker, Psychic Medium and Demonologist, Melinda has helped countless people from her home state, to the lower forty-eight

MELINDA KAY LYONS

-all the way to the astral realm. With more than twelve years of paranormal experiences, and a higher level of awareness of spirit, her developed relationship with the respect and understanding of the afterlife has changed the lives of many.

Melinda has been a guest on radio shows through iHeart Radio. Has been a recent guest on *Jim Harold's "The Paranormal Podcast Guy*, and with *The NewFoundland Paranormal Podcast*. She is also a host and daily vlogger on her official Youtube channel, *Last Frontier Medium*, where she goes within the depths of the other side while doing readings for clients for free.

Also By
Melinda Kay Lyons

Demons and Familiars

To embark on the study of Demonology is to set onto a road severely less traveled. This book covers red flags and the insights into the consciousness of a Demonic entity. Meant as a contemporary guide into the knowing of when one is in the presence of a Demonic energy. Covering a range of the many signs, answering the questions by countless victims and even skeptics. The information is not only a structure of tips when discerning the malevolent presence -also holds cosmic answers to your many questions.

Available at Amazon.com and BN.com (Barnes and Noble).

Printed by Amazon Italia Logistica S.r.l.
Torrazza Piemonte (TO), Italy